Financial Management

ESSENTIALS OF NURSING MANAGEMENT

Series Editor: Jill Baker

Increasingly, nurses have to perform managerial work in addition to direct patient care. Basic education does not prepare them for this, as is evidenced by growing concern among professionals. The *Essentials of Nursing Management* series is designed to solve this problem and to allay anxieties. The volumes assist readers to improve their managerial skills, as well as their understanding of what constitutes sound management practice.

June Girvin
Leadership and Nursing

Verena Tschudin *with* **Jane Schober**
Managing Yourself

Diana Sale
Quality Assurance

Matthew Cripps, Alan Stuttard and Geoffrey Woodhall
Financial Management

Annabel Broome
Managing Change

Essentials of Nursing Management
Series Standing Order:
ISBN: 1–4039–4597–7
(outside North America only)

You can receive future titles in this series as they are published, by placing a standing order. Please contact your bookseller, or, in the case of difficulty, write to us at the address below with your name and address, the title of the series, and the ISBN quoted above.

Customer Services Department, Palgrave Ltd, Houndmills, Basingstoke, Hampshire, RG21 6XS, England

---

ESSENTIALS OF NURSING MANAGEMENT

Financial Management

Budgeting in Hospitals and in Primary Care Trusts

Second Edition

Matthew Cripps
Alan Stuttard
Geoffrey Woodhall

First published 2005 by
PALGRAVE MACMILLAN
Houndmills, Basingstoke, Hampshire RG21 6XS and
175 Fifth Avenue, New York, N.Y. 10010
Companies and representatives throughout the world

PALGRAVE MACMILLAN is the global academic imprint of the Palgrave Macmillan division of St. Martin's Press, LLC and of Palgrave Macmillan Ltd. Macmillan® is a registered trademark in the United States, United Kingdom and other countries. Palgrave is a registered trademark in the European Union and other countries.

ISBN 1–4039–4530–6

This book is printed on paper suitable for recycling and made from fully managed and sustained forest sources.

A catalogue record for this book is available from the British Library.

10 9 8 7 6 5 4 3 2 1
14 13 12 11 10 09 08 07 06 05

Printed and bound in China

1004522274 T

Contents

List of Figures and Tables

Introduction

Sound financial management is a key requirement that underpins the successful delivery of modern health care.

Pamela Dyson, National Head of Finance Staff Development (NHS)

The sole purpose of this book is to give confidence to the reader. Finance is a specialised subject, but it is not an impossible one. Reading about finance is like learning to swim, taking one stroke at a time: learning when to breathe, when to push, when to glide forward: then forgetting all that and launching out. The water holds you up: you didn't believe that it could, but it can! Then you say 'Come on in, the water's lovely!' The sense of pride, of achievement, of satisfaction that something attempted has been demonstrated to work. In a similar way, finance will support your aims and plans. It takes time to feel confident, but each successful bid for resources will provide evidence that the system works. The first stroke may be on a computer screen, on a piece of paper, in the margin of a newspaper or journal; collectively these thoughts lead to reports, discussions, decisions, orders, staff, resources. The tangible benefits of finance being made available are a result of someone stepping out in a confident way. This book is designed to give you that level of confidence.

The book is also about caring: caring for patients, staff, employees, organisations, units, wards, resources and assets. The plans within which everyone has to work contain unfamiliar words, and the book seeks to explain and put in context the words used in the management of health care.

The book is also a bridge: taking the reader from a centralised system of management into a new era of devolved management. The new arrangements rely upon Primary Care Trusts having a very important role in the planning and commissioning of care. The reasons behind the introduction of foundation hospitals are explained.

Following the publication of the ten-year *NHS Plan* and *Delivering the NHS Plan*, the government embarked upon the largest programme of change within an organisation ever attempted anywhere in the world. The success of this programme depends on analysing patient pathways and making decisions at a local level, supported by rational arguments and clear, measurable plans.

There is great importance attached to the need for transparency, and greater emphasis on the quality of the patient experience. Health professionals will be working in a changing organisation, and will be empowered to take decisions at a local level, in organisations which are locally accountable and subject to scrutiny, monitoring, and regulation.

The book is based on the latest information available in 2004. Most chapters contain illustrations and website addresses where more information can be found. The authors wish to record their appreciation of the comments received from users of the First Edition, and the support and advice given by many people in the preparation of this edition. We hope that users of the book will write in with ideas and suggestions for future editions.

1

Structure of the NHS

In the UK, the government of the day has the power to change its policy by introducing new legislation in Parliament. In 1989 the government heralded the largest single set of reforms in the National Health Service (NHS) since 1948 by the publication of two White Papers in 1989; *Working for Patients* (DoH) and *Caring for People* (Secretaries of State for Health, Social Security) and a new structure was introduced with the NHS and Community Care Act, 1990. The structures set out in these documents have been amended with the publication of the Health Act 1999, *The NHS Plan*, published in 2000, and *Shifting the Balance of Power*, 2001.

The structure is headed by the Secretary of State for Health, who is answerable to Parliament, and has a place in the Cabinet.

The *Department of Health*, headed by the Secretary of State, employs a wide range of health professionals and technical experts with whom he may consult. It has responsibility for controlling the management of the health service through long and short-term plans, and by a continual overview of the service, including developing strategy and setting the objectives of the NHS.

Under the first set of reforms in 1990, the NHS Executive and its eight regional offices had the responsibility of monitoring the implementation of policies in the NHS. These regional offices have now been disbanded in the latest reforms (2001). Responsibility for policy and reporting to government ministers has passed back to the Department of Health.

Strategic Health Authorities (StHAs) have taken over the other responsibilities from regional offices, and also from the now disbanded health authorities. StHAs cover areas of more than a million population. Their responsibilities include the performance management of Primary Care Trusts (PCTs) and other Trusts to ensure that government targets are achieved.

a. Authority (performance management) from April 2002

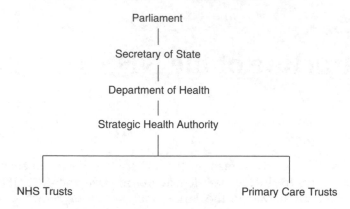

Parliament

Secretary of State

Department of Health

Strategic Health Authority

NHS Trusts   Primary Care Trusts

b. Funding (commissioning) from April 2003

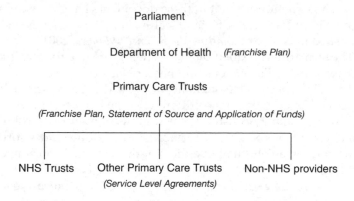

Parliament

Department of Health   *(Franchise Plan)*

Primary Care Trusts

(Franchise Plan, Statement of Source and Application of Funds)

NHS Trusts   Other Primary Care Trusts   Non-NHS providers
(Service Level Agreements)

Figure 1.1   The structure of the NHS and the flow of funds

PCTs have been established with the latest reforms. They have taken over the commissioning responsibilities, previously carried out by health authorities, as well as the provision of community and primary care services. In some areas PCTs provide learning difficulty and continuing care services. The role of PCTs is explained more fully in Chapter 9.

NHS Trusts are a result of the 1989/1991 reforms; they represent mental health and acute hospitals which have become self-governing. The structure is shown in Figure 1.1.

Financial Planning at a National Level

The money required to run the NHS represents the largest single category of expenditure in the budget of central government. As such it has to be closely planned and controlled, and approved by Parliament. Before receiving Parliamentary approval, the First Secretary of the Treasury has to negotiate with ministers about the claims of their departments for future spending. The Cabinet has to consider the rate of growth of different departments, and the Chancellor of the Exchequer has to assess the state of the economy and its ability to produce sufficient revenue from taxation to support all the government's spending proposals. The summary of these proposals is published as the 'Autumn Statement', and is an important indicator of the assumptions which have been built into the plans: for example, it draws attention to areas where 'new money' may be available for developing new services.

Planned expenditure is divided into two categories:

- *Current (or Revenue)* refers to on-going regular day-to-day spending on pay, salaries, supplies and expenses of the NHS.
- *Capital* refers to large schemes of construction, land purchase or buying vehicles and equipment, where the benefit from that spending will extend for a period beyond the year in which the spending actually occurred.

An example of how the government reports its own financial plans is shown in Table 1.1.

This extract from the government's own expenditure plans illustrates an important requirement of the health service: the need to summarise information to convey the totality of expenditure, the requirements on the public purse, and for health provision in the community. Throughout this book, you will find summaries of information, and the task of the accountant within the health service is to analyse, collate and summarise financial information. Hospitals prepare data which are given to business managers, who may delegate some of the responsibility to groups of physicians or

Table 1.1 Department of Health, central government's own expenditure 2002/03

	(£ millions)
Hospital, Community and Family Health Services	46,168
Capital Charges	1,697
Total available funding	47,86
Comprising:	
Centrally Funded Initiatives and Services and Special Allocations	6,397
Total for Strategic Health Authorities and Primary Care Trusts	41,468
	47,865

Source: 2002/03 Health Authority Revenue Resource Limits, England. Exposition Book, Department of Health

nurses within a directorate. Data are provided as an estimate, are analysed at the point where money is spent, and monitored subsequently to find out where variations have occurred between what is planned and what was spent. Data collection is useful at different levels of decision making: at the point of service delivery, at ward or clinic level, at directorate level, at hospital level, and at national level. People working within the health service need to have a common understanding at all levels so that they can communicate effectively.

Central government is aware that the provision of health services is a politically sensitive topic, because the government, through its plans and strategies, is affecting the lives of many people. As individuals, people want the right pattern of treatment and the right pattern of care when they become ill. The Cabinet has to balance the needs of health against the needs of other departments, for example education, defence, prisons, and so on. The Treasury acts as the data collecting agency through which all this financial information passes. A six-year summary of the totals of public expenditure between 1996/97 and 2001/02 is shown in Table 1.2.

A Treasury minister, the Chief Secretary to the Treasury, has to reconcile the government's political aspirations with the availability of funds through taxation, and has to communicate with departmental ministers, who are the politically appointed chiefs of spend-

Table 1.2 Public expenditure in the UK, 1996/97 to 2001/02 (in £ billions)

	96/97	97/98	98/99	99/00	00/01	01/02
Health	40.8	42.5	44.7	48.7	52.6	58.1
Education	36.4	37.4	39.0	40.9	44.1	50.1
Law & order	16.2	16.9	17.3	18.8	20.1	23.0
Transport	10.1	9.2	8.7	8.6	8.7	10.1
Environment	8.2	8.4	8.4	8.5	10.2	10.8
Housing	4.6	3.7	3.7	2.8	3.2	5.1

Source: Public Expenditure Statistical Analyses 2002–2003, Cm 5401,TSO,Table 3.3

ing departments, about the extent to which their spending needs and priorities will be met.

Some aspirations are met immediately, others are regarded as a priority and, over the life of a Parliament, both the Treasury ministers and the departmental ministers are accountable through Parliament for their strategies and decisions on service delivery and maintenance of standards within agreed spending patterns, authorised by Parliament. At the end of the Parliamentary term of office, usually every five years, the electorate has the opportunity of indicating its agreement or otherwise of the government's record and performance through a simple cross on a ballot paper.

In a democracy, the driving force which leads a person to vote may be a combination of reactions or feelings that the voter wants 'more of the same', or a positive change to 'something different', with the anticipation that a change is a 'change for the better'. In the period before an election, parties, both of government and opposition, will seek to put forward their plans as a manifesto, and each of these documents will be analysed publicly through the press, television and other media sources. Ultimately, voters will decide whether or not to use their vote, and which way to exercise it

While in office, the party of government can communicate its plans through consultation papers (known as *Green Papers*), or can make definite proposals for change (known as *White Papers*) and can issue press releases through the media, explaining present or proposed policies.

An opposition party can support, modify or oppose these proposals when they come to Parliamentary consideration, through the means of select committees or through the committee stage in

Parliament. The House of Commons in committee can give detailed consideration, line by line if necessary, to proposed legislation embodying government policy.

When Parliament is dissolved, and an election is pending, those processes cease, and the public at large is able to judge the merits of existing policies and the proposals put forward for the future in the parties' manifestos. We do not know what influences people to vote, but health, as the biggest single spending service, must feature somewhere in the public's perception of the government's overall performance. For this reason, health is a politically sensitive and important topic to the government of the day. The descriptions in the following pages of how the health service is organised reflect the current position at the time of writing. It is possible that changes may be made in the future to the structure and processes described.

Financial Planning at a Local Level

In order for the Department of Health to have an overview of finance, it is necessary for each StHA, PCT and NHS Trust to provide financial information. Following the reforms of 1991 and 1999, the responsibility for health care has been divided between 'commissioners' and 'providers'.

Commissioners

PCTs became responsible for assessing the needs of their resident populations, and securing health services for them. So the role of the PCTs was to review the health needs of their geographical areas, by research, by examining patterns of illness, patterns of care provided in the past, current caseloads and waiting lists, and through annual contracts, known as *Service Level Agreements* (SLAs) securing sufficient care for such a load to be handled within a twelve-month period, ending on 31 March. From April 2003 onwards, SLAs will include an initial agreement for the two years following the twelve-month period, so in total, projections of care will cover three years.

Providers

An NHS Trust hospital would be the main provider of health care for the commissioning PCTs. Trust hospitals would deliver services to 'commissioners' in accordance with a pre-arranged Service Level Agreement (SLA). The SLA would state the volume of patients to be treated, and would specify the quality of care and the quantity or amount of care to be provided.

Dual Role

The latest reforms cast PCTs in a dual role, as commissioner and provider. In their provider function, community services, such as district nursing, primary care, and learning difficulties, are managed by a PCT, both for their own residents and, via SLAs, the residents of neighbouring PCTs.

In their commissioning function, PCTs commission both from mental health and acute NHS Trusts and from neighbouring PCTs, as well as non-NHS providers. This aspect is discussed in more detail in Chapter 10.

Managed Competition

The separation of responsibilities between 'commissioner' and 'providers' in the 1990 Act introduced the practice of managed competition into the health service. This was brought to an end in 1998. However, the Patient Choice Initiative (2002) has reintroduced competition. The initiative allows patients to choose to be treated by NHS Trusts other than their local provider, the private sector, or even by foreign health care. This choice will be made available where the local Trust cannot provide care within a specified timescale or where an operation is cancelled. This means that local Trusts will compete in order not to lose 'custom' to other providers and will also seek to provide care where other Trusts cannot meet their timescales. The introduction of 'managed competition' meant that the provision of health care was not going to be a free-for-all, in which unrestrained market forces could permanently destabilise the provision of care, which had taken many years to develop, but instead, competition was to be introduced steadily and gradually. The existence of SLAs strengthens the information available to PCTs as commissioners and creates a stronger planning environment in which information on activity within the NHS would be passed to the DoH via the StHA.

NHS Trusts

A Trust is a self-governing unit within the NHS, but independent of a PCT or StHA. A Trust earns its income from SLAs, and retains any financial surplus as a result of its income being greater than its expenditure in any financial year. The reverse also applies: a Trust may incur a deficit if its expenditure is greater than its income in any financial year. A Trust has a duty to break even over a three-year period; so, any surpluses or deficits have to be considered over a three-year period, and action needs to be taken to ensure that deficits are recovered and that the overall effect is evenly balanced. A Trust is not confined to a hospital: other aspects of the NHS can apply for Trust status, for example:

- ambulance services
- services for a particular group, such as patients with mental illness or mental handicap
- a single, major acute hospital

Each Trust has a line or a duty of direct accountability through the StHA to the Secretary of State for Health. They are independent of commissioner management. They have perpetual succession: that is, they are an independent legal entity, with power to determine policies, and to monitor the execution of those policies in line with agreed guidelines and government targets.

Business Plans for NHS Trusts

As a Trust is independently governed, but is within the NHS, it has to report to the StHA and prepare an annual business plan covering three years. The plans must show:

- the assumptions about the purchasing power of the authorities with whom the Trust has contractual arrangements
- plans for future capital developments and how these will be funded
- assumptions about changes in external conditions, for example patient numbers, inflation, interest rates.

The StHA will be able to assess over a period of years how closely a

Trust is performing in comparison to its plans, and will be able to form an opinion on the accuracy or reliability of plans from each Trust.

Income estimates are based on the volume of expected work multiplied by the price of each item of service.

Expenditure estimates are based on accurate costing of each function or clinical specialism. The process of building up a budget is explained in Chapter 6.

Types of Contract

In order to establish a contractual relationship between 'purchaser' and 'provider', three main types of contract are available and in regular use in the NHS.

Block Contract

This indicates the types of service to be provided, and an annual contract price, payable in instalments, entitling the purchaser to refer patients within the area of the PCT to the provider for treatment.

Cost and Volume Contract

This is similar to a block contract but has an indication of volume, permitting the commissioner and the provider to renegotiate for any excess caseload after a contract limit has been reached. As experience grows of numbers of patients and referrals, PCTs may choose to express their contracts more in terms of 'cost and volume', in preference to block contracts.

Non-Contract Work

A small proportion of hospital work is not covered by contracts. These cases are known as Out of Area Treatments (OATs). The cases tend to be arising from emergencies, and have to be paid for by the 'home' PCT, that is, the PCT in whose area the patient resides. Data and statistics are collected about the extent of OATs, and providers are funded on the basis of what happened two years previously. This reduces the administrative burden of the previous system (which was known as extra-contractual referrals or ECRs), and provides funding to providers on historical data.

Example of Out of Area Treatments
An acute Trust hospital may provide OATS to PCT 1 and PCT 2 in financial Year 1. In Year 3, the Trust receives funding from PCT 1 and PCT 2 (based on the work it did two years previously), but the provider may in Year 3 actually be giving care to patients and cases from PCT 3 and PCT 4. It will be two years further on, in financial Year 5, that the Trust will receive funding from PCT 3 and PCT 4.

The stages leading to an SLA are illustrated in Figure 1.2

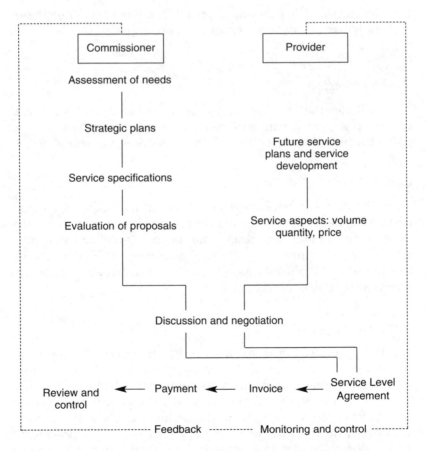

Figure 1.2   Stages leading to a Service Level Agreement

Further Reading

Corry D (ed) (1997) *Public Expenditure, Effective Management and Control.* The Dryden Press, London.

Department of Health (1989) *Working for Patients* Cm 555, DoH, London.

Department of Health (2000) *The NHS Plan,* DoH, London.

Department of Health (2001) *Modernising the NHS: Shifting the Balance of Power,* DoH, London.

Department of Health (2002) *Delivering the NHS Plan,* Cm 5503, DoH, London.

Department of Health (2003) *Building on the Best: Choice, Responsiveness and Equity in the NHS,* Cm 6079, DoH, London.

Department of Health (2004) *The NHS Improvement Plan: Putting People at the Heart of Public Services,* Cm 6268, DoH, London.

NHS and Community Care Act 1990 and the Health Act 1999. An annually updated summary of changes in health service policy can be found in the *Public Services Yearbook,* published by Pitman, in which there is a Programme Review chapter on health.

Secretaries of State for Health, Social Security, Wales and Scotland (1989) *Curing for People: Community Care in the Next Decade and Beyond,* Cm 849, HMSO,London.

Useful Websites

www.dh.gov.uk/shiftingthebalance
www.dh.gov.uk/shiftingthebalance/haconsultation
www.dh.gov.uk/nhsplan
www.nhsuk/thenhsexplained/priorities.asp
www.dh.gov.uk/deliveringthenhsplan/index
www.dh.gov.uk/nhsfinancialreforms/sla_guidance
www.dh.gov.uk/allocations/exposition

2

The Planning and Control of Capital Expenditure: Preparing Capital Estimates

Introduction

In Chapter 1 it was pointed out that the UK government prepared plans for its activities, and differentiated between 'capital' spending and 'current' spending. Capital is a term which is widely used, and indicates that the purpose of the spending is long term: the benefits of acquiring a capital item, such as a health centre, will spread over future years, and the initial cost represents an investment which enables the authority making that investment to continue to function and extend its services. This chapter looks at the way capital spending is planned, co-ordinated, and judged, in the competitive environment of different schemes competing for scarce resources.

Current Expenditure

'Current expenditure' is a term which is used in central government planning; it means the day-to-day expenditure which pays for items such as salaries, wages, supplies, costs of running a service, including office costs, telephones, stationery, and so on.

'Current' is treated separately from 'capital' because traditionally in the planning of governments, current spending represented the ongoing commitments and had to be financed each year; capital was more problematic, and needed different considerations.

Planning for Capital

Planning for capital expenditure is usually done at a high level within an organisation, and requires a multidisciplinary approach. The product of planning remains for a long time; for example, district general hospitals may have been planned 20 years ago, or longer: the buildings were planned on the requirements and procedures followed at that time; medical practice will have changed in the intervening period. The length of stay may have shortened due to advances in clinical or diagnostic practice. Care may be outside the hospital, in the community, or under the supervision of the GP, with supporting practice-based staff, rather than hospital-based staff, and consequently the buildings which were 'inherited' may not fully reflect the present needs, workloads, or present day case mix. So many proposals for capital expenditure arise from service needs, to amend, to alter, to adapt buildings. A scheme will probably start as a suggestion from a department, if changes in current practice are needed. Architects or planners will be invited to do a 'space utilisation' survey or report, and some proposals will be made to alter or adapt the layout of the floor, the position of entrances, the siting of partitions and equipment. Planners will design a number of alternative layouts or solutions, commonly called 'options', and these will be costed. This is not an exercise in precision, but rather an estimate in rough terms of what money might be needed to be set aside to complete the envisaged scheme.

Contract Terms

Some of the terms used at the estimate stage may already be familiar to readers.

Prime Sum

This is a figure to ensure that a particular item is not overlooked, but the figure does not guarantee that the item can be bought for that amount. For example, if a scheme was for building a day room at a hospital, and a TV was required, a prime sum may be included in the estimate showing 'TV £500'. This is to indicate that the actual selection of the set is something which is going to happen at a later date, and it may be regarded as part of the scheme, but at the discretion of the manager involved. Thus, in making the actual purchase, the budget holder may opt for a particular style and size, and the outcome may be that a set is bought for £800, and so the extra £300 would have to be found from some other budget; that is, outside the amount provided by or asked for in the capital scheme submission. One way of describing a prime sum is to say it is a 'first guess'.

Provisional Sum

This is an amount which is included in the cost of a scheme, but is a guess, and when the work is actually done, then the true cost will be charged on a basis which has been agreed beforehand in the contract agreement. For example, if a new radiography department was being built, requiring an electricity supply, the work of laying new cable to the site and its entry to the building would probably be estimated in advance, based on the distance the cable had to travel. That calculation would therefore be a 'provisional sum'. When the work was carried out, it is possible that the electricity company would either do the work, or sub-contract it to a contractor, and the work would be charged to the hospital according to a schedule of charges or rates; for example, to cover the different stages of the work; digging out a trench, supplying labour of different skills, hire of machinery, cost of cable, and so on. So the final bill would supersede the 'provisional sum' which had been included in the planning stage, and the final bill may be greater than the 'provisional sum', consequently, some extra finance would be needed. Provisional sums are items which cannot be estimated with accuracy in advance of the work being carried out; and the true cost may be dependent upon factors not known at the time the design stage is being prepared, for example, ground conditions, physical conditions of the site affecting type of foundations, or other imponderables, such as uncertainty about the extent of the work required.

Costing a Capital Scheme

A proposal for a capital scheme will be 'costed', that is money values will be attached to various elements or parts of the work, and, as a result of different skills and techniques being involved, the scheme may appear to be 'owned' by professionals who are outside the department which originated the scheme. So in justifying or presenting the reasons for the scheme, the sponsoring or initiating department will need to be able to explain the different stages and components, and will need to be fully briefed on what has happened to the scheme in all stages of its preparation.

If the scheme is successful in being supported for funding, then it will go forward for inclusion in an annual capital programme. This is an indication that the scheme has satisfied the criteria laid down by the Trust or district authority for inclusion in the programme. Normally, submissions have to be 'standardised' into a particular format for presentation to management and to the policy-making body of the Trust or district authority.

For example, as well as a narrative report which is used to acquaint directors and non-executive members, a table of figures would be prepared to summarise the main elements of cost for which approval was being sought. At the same time, the sponsoring or initiating department would have to indicate the duration of the proposed contract, so that capital finance, the money available to pay for it, could be timed to be raised at the appropriate time to meet the payments. This is known as the 'phasing of capital expenditure payments'.

At the stage of putting these details forward for consideration for inclusion in a capital programme, the department may have to wait its turn until other on-going schemes have been completed, and there is room within the authority's forward plans for a scheme of this size. It is not unusual for a scheme to be approved in principle for inclusion at a later date, when funds allow. What then happens to the figures already prepared which may become out of date due to the passage of time and inflationary pressures on the cost of materials and on wage rates? Generally, a capital expenditure spending proposal is costed out at a certain point in time, and then subsequently the original figures are increased by the use of approved indices which reflect movements in prices. Within the construction industry, architects have access to generally accepted trade price indices, which produce information on a month-by-month basis. When the authority gives the approval for the scheme to go out to tender, a 'bill of quantities' is prepared. In the case of a construction contract, the bill of quantities analyses the requirements in detail, and contractors bidding for the scheme will build up a figure of cost from their own internal knowledge of current prices. The authority or person letting the contract will be able to judge whether the full cost of the contract comes within the amount already envisaged as being the total cost already approved by the authority.

An example of a scheme presented for approval, showing the elements of cost described in the text is shown in Table 2.1.

Schemes of this size are controlled by Strategic Health Authorities and by Primary Care Trusts (PCTs) or by architects contracted to the health authority. They had access to design teams, to specialist advice on planning, and to computer systems to cope with the planning and control of expenditure. Since the health service reforms, Trusts follow departmental guidelines relating to capital proposals.

Increasingly, the provision of health care is being influenced by new players in the provision of capital finance. In the 1980s central government channelled some health finance through local authori-

Table 2.1   Example of a large capital expenditure proposal

Scheme: Construction of an 80 flat nurses' home at a teaching hospital

| | | Phasing of expenditure | |
	Total cost £000s	*Year 1 £000s*	*Year 2 £000s*	*Year 3 £000s*
Purchase of site	800	800		
Foundations and site works	320	320		
Construction costs	3,840		3,500	340
Fitting out				
Internal fittings, equipment	130		90	40
Internal services, incl. heating	190			190
Furnishings and furniture	220			220
Total cost estimated at Year 1 prices	**5,500**	**1,120**	**3,590**	**790**
If the actual start was delayed three years, then the next report would have the Year 1 figures raised by the effects of price changes, e.g. increase in prices and costs between Year 1 and Year 3 is estimated as adding to the cost as follows				
(10 per cent uplift assumed)	550	112	359	79
Revised total cost	**6,050**	**1,232**	**3,949**	**869**

ties, and schemes for joint provision between local councils and district authorities were common. In the 1990s 'Care in the Community' has redefined whole areas of care, and, to meet the different patterns of care, money has been diverted by central government in such a way that agencies and authorities which were previously large participants in schemes have had their role redefined, and others have come on to the scene, with different methods, different approaches, and different financial traditions. Using 'Care of the Elderly' as an example, professional nurses in that area are likely to find an interaction at their level between health care, provided by Trust and hospitals, community care, offered by local authorities through social services, and increasingly more provision by the private sector, through nursing homes, run either privately or through companies. Some developments may be jointly financed, a mixture of publicly funded provision and private investment capital.

Interim and Final Certificates for Payments to Contractors

Not all schemes are large ones. Clearly, a sponsoring authority has to take great care over the ways in which schemes are put forward, and their physical progress. Much of the work is in the hands of contractors, who require payments as the schemes progress. These are known as 'stage' payments, or 'payments on account', and are based on the completion of certificates, signed by an architect or a quantity surveyor, to indicate that a certain percentage of the total work has been completed. Ultimately, a 'final' certificate is released which grants the balance of the contract monies to the contractor, when all the work covered by the contract has been done to the client's satisfaction. Sometimes, contracts proceed more slowly than expected, or may be completed more quickly than expected. Reasons for delay can include access to the site being delayed by planning enquiries, objections to development, difficult ground conditions, frost or adverse weather, unavailability of components or of specialised equipment. Fast progress can be caused by good weather conditions, good design, in which different trades can work simultaneously instead of waiting for different stages to be completed or the use of integrated components (for example, interior partitions or walls being factory made and incorporating both external finishes and interior wiring for electrics and internal services).

Cash Limits in Capital Schemes

In a situation where a PCT or Trust has a large capital programme, the finance for it will be determined in advance and usually this is 'cash limited', meaning a fixed sum is available, and no more. So, the monitoring of actual payments made under contracts is vitally important, to ensure that the 'cash limit' is not exceeded. If schemes are temporarily held up, it may be possible to substitute schemes close to the end of the financial year, to use up the available capital finance, and sometimes small schemes are prepared in readiness for what is known as 'slippage' in large schemes. 'Slippage' is where an existing scheme's payments are not going to fall exactly in the year in which they were expected, so there may be a 'shortfall' of payments in one year (for example money not spent as the scheme was not up to date), and when it is completed, there could be an 'excess' or 'overspending' in a following year, when the backlog of payments has to be made, including the shortfall from previous years. For this reason, the best capital programmes are those which include a combination of large and small schemes, and have some in readiness in case remedial action needs to be taken in the last months of a financial year. Sometimes, an authority is accused of having a 'spending spree' in the last months of its financial year, that is February and March, but, upon investigation, these often turn out to be new schemes being placed into the programme to ensure that the allocation of capital money for the year is not lost.

Small Capital Schemes: Example

The criteria for a small scheme may be substantially different from a large scheme. Small schemes usually involve expenditure of £5,000 or more. Ideally, they should offer different ways of providing service in a more cost-effective way; in other words, a small spending of capital should be a forerunner of better conditions, or better outcomes in patient care.

The following is an example of a small capital expenditure proposal, and the way in which it is justified.

The area covered by PCT X is 20 miles from north to south, and 12 miles from east to west. Most of the population is concentrated in the central area. In the community services, a doctor is employed to run a clinic on Mondays and Tuesdays in the north, and on Thursdays and Fridays in the south, at two health centres. Wednesdays are spent visiting schools on a rota basis, to hold occasional clinics, but these are very sporadic, and judged not to be totally satisfactory.

As the majority of the referrals to the service come from the centre, they have to travel between eight and ten miles to a clinic: there is no central provision. The doctor's appointments involve the doctor in a fair amount of travelling which is regarded as time wasted.

A capital expenditure proposal has come from the service: adapt a waiting area in one of the central clinics, and use the area so released as a new clinic for the doctor for two days per week (see Table 2.2). One clinic session in the north would be cancelled, leaving the doctor's pattern of attendances as: Monday north; Tuesday and Wednesday central; Thursday and Friday south.

Table 2.2   Example of a small capital expenditure proposal

Capital costs involved	
	£
Building of partitions, new door and walls	10,000
Desk, furniture and computer	5,500
Decoration and fitting carpets	2,000
Total capital cost	**17,500**

If the scheme went ahead, the PCT would not be involved in any additional revenue expenditure. No extra people are being employed as a result of this proposal. The PCT would benefit from a reduction in the doctor's travelling expenses. If centrally based for two days, the doctor would not be travelling on those days.

The present budget covers the annual costs of two days in the north clinic: 20-mile round trip for two days times, say, 45 weeks; and two days in the south clinic: 20-mile round trip for two days times, say, 45 weeks.

The new revenue budget would be based on one day in the north clinic (20 miles); two days in the central location with negligible travelling (assuming that the doctor was nominally attached to the central location); and two days in the south as before.

This sort of proposal results in what is known as an 'efficiency saving'. By rearranging the present pattern of provision, and moving the resource (in this case the doctor) to the place where it is needed most (in the central area, where most of the caseload comes from), some costs can be cut out, for example travelling to less than full clinics in the north, and school visits which are regarded as not as effective or as satisfactory as a clinic attendance. The long-term result of this rearrangement is that the potential of the doctor to attend to cases is increased, because more space has been made available by the use of partitions in an existing building, and other space (in the north on Tuesdays) has been released for other purposes.

Efficiency Savings

An 'efficiency saving' is one whereby altering procedures or practice enables more work to be done with fewer resources; in the case of the doctor, the time in the north was not fully accounted for; there was not the demand locally to use up every clinic session: consequently, by moving to the centre, the doctor was able to handle a better flow of cases, and see them closer to their normal location, and not involve them in time spent travelling. With an appointments system, better use could be made of the waiting area releasing room for seeing patients. The annual caseload handled by the doctor was potentially greater under the new system than if the old pattern of clinics had continued.

Is the proposal 'cost effective'? Yes, it appears to be, because the result of altering a central location to house these sorts of referrals has been that the number of cases with appointments each year will be greater than that under the present system. Part of the increase in efficiency is caused by giving the doctor a base out of which to work, instead of travelling to different locations each Wednesday; other efficiencies arise from cutting down the time spent behind the wheel of a car travelling between clinics. The service becomes more effective in the sense that the waiting time for these patients will reduce as more appointments are being made available.

This is an example of a small scheme which has a good chance of being successfully included in a capital programme, for these reasons:

1. It produces greater efficiency, in terms of higher potential throughput of cases, due to the doctor being available at new locations.
2. It is relatively straightforward to implement; no new staff are required.
3. It results in better effectiveness within the service; more clients are reached, without increasing costs, other than small increases in postage and telephones, which would have occurred in the provision of more appointments.

In putting a proposal such as this forward, the main things to remember are these:

1. You need to find out whether this would be regarded as a 'capital' proposal, or a 'revenue' proposal. In this case, as it involves expenditure of over £5,000 in total, it would be classed as 'capital'. Different authorities may, from time to time, adjust the limit for 'capital' expenditure.
2. The scheme needs to be 'costed', that is an estimate of the work requiring to be done, in terms of capital costs.
3. You need to examine and present information on the impact of this proposal on other budget holders, and, in particular, you need to consider the possible consequences of capital expenditure: in this example, there would be savings from other expenditure headings, for example, transport costs, travelling expenses.
4. How far does the proposal fit in with the stated aims of the PCT? If, for example, it produces 'efficiency savings', then its case for inclusion in the capital programme will be strengthened.
5. Will it have any 'knock-on effects'? What other aspects of the service may be affected by this change of routine?

Up to this point, small capital schemes have been considered. Many of the considerations in a small scheme apply in the case of a large scheme, but with extra constraints, for example:

● A large scheme may have a long planning period before it becomes fully clear what is required.

- Expenditure may be difficult to justify in competition with other demands from other departments.
- Priorities may be difficult to establish. For example, one department may be seen to be more hard pressed than another, and difficult choices may have to be made by managers and decision makers.

SELF-STUDY QUESTIONS

1. How would you define 'current expenditure'?

2. What is 'capital expenditure', and where would you find the rules relating to it in your organisation?

3. Distinguish between a 'prime sum' and a 'provisional sum' in a contract.

Further Reading

Allen MW and Myddelton DR (1992) *Essential Management Accounting*, 2nd edn, Prentice Hall, Hemel Hempstead.

Jones R and Pendlebury M (1996) *Public Sector Accounting*, 4th edn, Pitman Publishing, London.

3

Methods of Capital Appraisal

Introduction

In Chapter 2 the work of a capital planning team was described, outlining how a multidisciplinary team put together a proposal for a large scheme, having been through the process of identifying needs and priorities. This process culminates in the preparation of a series of reports, some of which are supported by financial information, such as the costs and phasings of money required to pay for the work involved, and an indication of the running costs of any new proposal.

What happens if two or more schemes come forward, and the ability of the authority is limited by cash shortages, and lack of funds? How can you judge the most suitable scheme to go forward in conditions of rationing of available funds?

The solution to this problem may be helped by the use of one or more capital appraisal techniques. The term 'capital appraisal' could be paraphrased and defined as 'the use of a series of tests which results in one scheme becoming more favoured than others on the grounds of its financial attractiveness, assuming that in any final decision the non-financial factors are studied carefully, so that the decision is taken on operational and the service requirements' needs, and that the financial attractiveness of the scheme commends or supports the decision to adopt a particular solution'.

Capital Appraisal

Three different capital appraisal techniques are going to be explained which are widely used in the private sector. They offer assistance in the decision-making process, and ultimately the final decision depends on judgement and sensitivity to service-based issues. The financial techniques are as follows:

1. the accounting rate of return
2. the payback method
3. discounted cash flow (of which there is more than one technique: but the net present value method will be illustrated).

Example Using Three Different Project Appraisal Methods

A hospital Trust in the Midlands is able to spend £100,000 next year on a capital scheme, but is undecided about which of three projects should be undertaken. In all cases, there are sensitive local issues involved, and the Trust wishes to consider the financial implications of each scheme before coming to a final decision.

The costs and expected returns from each project are shown in Table 3.1.

Table 3.1   Costs and expected returns from three capital projects

End of year	Project A	Project B	Project C
Initial outlay Year 0	£100,000	£100,000	£100,000
Cash inflows			
Year 1	10,000	40,000	30,000
2	20,000	35,000	30,000
3	25,000	30,000	30,000
4	30,000	20,000	30,000
5	35,000		25,000
6	35,000		20,000
TOTAL	**155,000**	**125,000**	**165,000**

Project A is an automated car park barrier and video surveillance system on the visitors' car park at the main hospital. Because of local opposition to the idea of making charges for parking at the hospital, their introduction is going to be phased in gradually.

Project B is a scheme to upgrade a conference suite at the hospital, and make it available for outside bookings. It is expected to have a very good initial response, but income may decline from Year 4 onwards due to the opening of a new hotel in close proximity to the hospital, which may attract trade away from the conference suite.

Project C is a refurbishment of bedrooms in nurses' accommodation owned by the Trust, and would result in higher rentals being earned for the improved accommodation.

So, using money as a common measurement in all three projects, it may be possible to compare their respective returns, from the point of view of the Trust. They all cost the same amount of 'capital', that is £100,000, but produce different amounts of revenue to the Trust:

> 'A' brings in £155,000 over six years
> 'B' brings in £125,000 over four years
> 'C' brings in £165,000 over six years

Judging on money values only, Project C seems the best return as it brings in the most. The technique known as the 'accounting rate of return' can be used in situations such as this, to highlight the differences between projects.

So if the Trust wanted to maximise its return on its outlay of £100,000, it would opt for the highest figure (10.8 per cent) and adopt Project C in preference to the other two.

To rank them in order of preference, the results would be:

	Project
First	C
Second	A
Third	B

The figures would be drawn up as shown in Table 3.2.

Table 3.2 Accounting rate of return

	Option 'A' £	Option 'B' £	Option 'C' £
Total amount 'earned' by the scheme	155,000	125,000	165,000
Subtract the initial cost of the scheme	100,000	100,000	100,000
Surplus of income over costs	**55,000**	**25,000**	**65,000**
Divide by the period in years over which this surplus is earned	6 years	4 years	6 years
gives an annual return of	£9,166	£6,250	£10,833
gives an 'annual accounting rate of return' of... on the initial investment of £100,000	9.2%	6.3%	10.8%

The accounting rate of return has a number of practical disadvantages as an appraisal method:

1. It fails to recognise the 'time value of money'. This will be explained later in the chapter when discounting methods are described.
2. It can be adversely affected by different rates of depreciation used by different classes of assets.
3. It can produce the 'wrong' recommendation when compared to other appraisal methods.

Consequently it is of limited use only, and then only if supported by other more reliable methods. It may be used in commercial situations where the rate of return is considered an important element in a capital decision. In the National Health Service the opportunities for its use are very limited, as other more important criteria apply, such as clinical priorities and investment for improved patient care.

The 'Payback Method' of Capital Appraisal

In a situation where capital money is in short supply, the managers of a hospital may feel that one of their priorities is to divert any capital money available into projects which will have a quick return. The illustration of the accounting rate of return depended upon working out the average rate of revenue arising from the project as the criterion for going ahead: the 'payback method' concentrates its attention not on revenues, but on the speed in which the original investment is recovered, on the grounds that, the speedier the return, the more projects can in fact be financed through using the money which returns to the organisation once again.

Using the same figures of cash inflows, that is income arising from each project before charging depreciation, the payback method seeks to determine *when* the flow of revenues equals the amount of the original investment of £100,000. How soon does the original £100,000 come back?

> In project A, it is slightly less than 4½ years
> In B, it is about 2¾ years
> In C, it is 3⅓ years

So, the quickest return is achieved by choosing Project B.

The rankings under the payback method would be:

	Project
First	B
Second	C
Third	A

The following are the main disadvantages of the payback method:

1. It fails to recognise the beneficial effect of positive flows which occur after the payback time, for example, Project C has the biggest return in total, yet comes only second in the ranking, not first.
2. Payback tends to disadvantage projects which move slowly at the outset, but which gain momentum later in terms of earnings.
3. Payback assumes that speed of recovering the original capital investment is more important than other considerations, for

example, it tends to ignore the profit potential at the expense of or in preference to the speed of turning over capital.

Discounted Cash Flow Techniques

In general, the use of discounted cash flow techniques is more favoured than either accounting rate of return or payback. Both of these techniques have disadvantages to the operational manager.

Discounting brings into the consideration of options the time value of money. This is a way of recognising that the flow of money in the future will be influenced by matters such as the passage of time, and the method seeks to recognise this in its assumptions and methodology.

What is the time effect of money? The project is assumed to be built in a 'year of outlay', known as Year 0.

Cash inflows are expected at the end of each subsequent year: 12 months after Year 0, we have the first revenue arising, called Year 1. Revenue is assumed to come in on the final day of that year; the next year's revenue comes in at Year 2, again, on the final day of that year.

The profile of spending and receipts is shown in Table 3.3.

Table 3.3   Spending and receipts profile

Year 0	Year 1	Year 2
Initial outlay or investment in the project	First money or income received	Second amount of money received

The technique of 'discounting' looks at the amounts and timing of future cash flows, and expresses them in terms of the start of the project. Does the future revenue justify the investment at the beginning? How do we bring future revenues into the reckoning? Basically, future money is estimated at the time it occurs, then is expressed as a figure which if invested at the start of the project at a known rate of interest, would produce the actual amount of revenue expected at the specified future date. Most management accounting texts and some computer software products contain the mathematical figures you need for such a calculation.

Example of Net Present Value

If we assume that an organisation can borrow money at a cost of 10 per cent per annum, we can use discounting tables to decide whether any capital expenditure proposal is worthwhile. The discounting factors which we need will be described in the tables or software as 'present value figures of £1 received after a period of years at 10 per cent'.

The factors for 10 per cent are as follows:

After 1 year	.9091
2 years	.8264
3 years	.7513

So, assuming that you made an investment of £2,400 in Year 0, and it produced £1,000 income in each of three successive years, and the cost of borrowing money to your organisation was 10 per cent per annum, would the investment produce sufficient revenue to justify the initial outlay?

Method: Show the original outlay in Year 0

Year 0	£2,400

Then record the revenue received in each year

Income Year 1	£1,000
Year 2	£1,000
Year 3	£1,000

Apply the appropriate discount factor from tables, in this case the cost of capital to the organisation is 10 per cent, so the 10 per cent factor would be used (see Table 3.4).

Table 3.4 Net present value

Year	Revenue	Factor @ 10%	Multiply revenue by the factor
Year 1	£1,000	.9091	£909
Year 2	£1,000	.8264	£826
Year 3	£1,000	.7513	£751

Total discounted revenue is	£2,486
Subtract the value of the initial outlay	£2,400
which leaves a positive residual amount of	£86

Provided the residual amount at the end of the project's life is positive, then the project is worth proceeding with, and is worth supporting as it covers its cost and the cost of borrowing the capital to undertake it. If the final result is negative, then the revenues do not justify the outlay involved.

The use of discounting methods, such as discounted cash flow, is regarded as being more sophisticated than other methods of capital appraisal, such as the accounting rate of return and the payback method.

The element of sophistication comes from the fact that discounting takes into consideration the life of a project over a specified period of time, and takes into account the time value of money, that is, the fact that money becomes eroded in its purchasing power over the passage of time. For that reason, discounting methods are preferable to the accounting rate of return method, or the payback method, as neither of these allows for the time value of money.

In preparing a mathematical approach to a problem, you should remember the basic assumptions, and make these clear to people using the appraisal as a basis for decision making. Some things are not capable of being measured in terms of money, such as efficiency savings, or saving in waiting time, or reduction in the length of waiting lists, and these items need to be mentioned alongside the financial results of appraisals, so that the non-financial elements of a decision are apparent as well as the financial information.

Returning to the appraisal for Projects A, B, and C, we can use discounted cash flow or net present value techniques. Assume in this situation that the cost of capital required to finance this scheme would be 12 per cent per annum, so a factor of 12 per cent would be used (see Table 3.5).

Table 3.5 Calculations of the discounted value (net present value)

Factor at 12% Revenue A £	Discounted value £	Revenue B £	Discounted value £	Revenue C £	Discounted value £
.8929 10,000	8,929	40,000	35,716	30,000	26,787
.7929 20,000	15,858	35,000	27,752	30,000	23,787
7118 25,000	17,705	00,000	21,354	30,000	21,354
.6355 30,000	19,065	20,000	12,710	30,000	19,065
.5674 35,000	19,859			25,000	14,185
.5066 35,000	17,731			20,000	10,132
	99,237		97,532		115,310
Deduct initial outlay of	100,000		100,000		100,000
Result	**−(763)**		**−(2,468)**		**15,310**
	Negative		**Negative**		**Positive (this would be the preferred option)**

Under the accounting rate of return method C came out best.

Under payback, the results favoured B as it had the quickest return of the original investment.

Under discounting methods, the rating was

	Project
First	C
Second	A
Third	B

Discounting methods seem to be the most suitable for capital appraisal, and match more closely than the other methods the commercial considerations of those whose capital is at risk. They have been used in the health service for the appraisal of capital projects, and proposals usually adopt a 'test discount rate' which is specified in Department of Health guidelines. The test discount rate is a specified rate of interest as recommended at the time by the Treasury in view of current interest rate conditions and it is used to compare the effect of mutually exclusive projects. In the private sector, the opportunity cost of capital is substituted for the test discount rate.

Capital proposals therefore represent an important part of preparing for the future development of services. The steps described in this chapter have emphasised that the initial stages are ones of close co-operation between different professionals: the capital proposal becomes multifaceted; the reports which describe its adoption need to be informative, and should be based on a careful consideration of all the options available.

The mathematics or accounting associated with such proposals is not too difficult; but, there are circumstances where some techniques are not appropriate, and the user needs to be aware of the limitations inherent in some of the techniques used.

SELF-STUDY QUESTIONS

1. What is slippage in a capital contract?

2. How useful is the payback method of capital appraisal and what are its disadvantages over other methods?

3. Describe the use of the accounting rate of return as a guide to capital investment.

4. What are the benefits of using discounted cash flow (net present value) in a capital appraisal compared with other techniques (for example payback)?

Further Reading

Allen MW and Myddelton DR (1992) *Essential Management Accounting*, 2nd edn, Prentice Hall, Hemel Hempstead.

Davies DB (1997) *The Art of Managing Finance*, 3rd edn, McGraw-Hill, Maidenhead.

Holmes P (1998) *Investment Appraisal*, International Thomson Business Press, London.

Mott G (1993) *Investment Appraisal*, M and E Handbook Series, 2nd edn, Pitman Publishing, London.

4

Sources of Capital Finance: Paying for Capital Expenditure Schemes and Capital Allocation

Introduction

This chapter examines some of the sources of capital available to the National Health Service. It also looks at some of the alternative ways of providing finance for capital projects.

Sources of Funds

Unconditional or Block Capital

Each year NHS Trusts and PCTs are notified of a sum of capital money which they are able to spend on their own schemes. In the case of NHS Trusts this is done via the external financing limit (EFL) and in the case of PCTs via an allocation of resources.

The main aim behind unconditional capital is that it should be used to maintain the NHS asset base. The amount each Trust receives is determined by reference to the turnover of the Trust and the depreciation value of the assets. However, it is not a uniform approach across the country and the Strategic Health Authorities are allowed discretion in how they apply the formula.

The sorts of items that the money will be spent on include:

● replacement medical equipment

- information technology
- health and safety
- major maintenance of building and plant.

Inevitably, some Trusts will choose to buy new things with the money but a balance must be kept between maintaining existing services and assets and developing new ones. With medical equipment it is also true that replacement items will include new and improved technology.

The process by which each Trust decides what the money will be spent on will vary but typically there may be sub-groups to look at each of the major headings. Departments within the Trust will be asked to submit bids to meet their own requirements. These bids will almost certainly exceed the money available and some system of prioritisation will be needed. This is particularly important in respect of any purchases, particularly of equipment, to ensure that there is no financial penalty to be incurred if a piece of equipment is replaced before the end of its useful life. Taking a vehicle as an example, if you replace your own car before you have paid off the loan you will still have the financial consequences of the balance of the loan to pay off. The same is true of any outstanding depreciation on assets which remain as a cost in the books of Trusts and PCTs.

Conditional or Discretionary Capital

In addition to the annual sum of unconditional capital, Trusts and PCTs will have the opportunity to bid the Strategic Health Authorities for additional sums of money for large new capital projects or for schemes which exceed their delegated limit. Such bids will need to be supported by a business case, which is a detailed document setting out the service and financial issues and containing an option appraisal of the proposed investment.

The level of delegation is determined by reference to the turnover of the Trust or PCT. Schemes with a value above the delegated limit have to be submitted for approval.

For NHS Trusts the sums involved are likely to exceed their internal resources to fund such schemes and therefore Trusts will be allowed to borrow funds to finance the scheme if it is to be financed from public funds. The money will then be repaid over a period of time in the form of a loan. An alternative (discussed in the next section) is to explore the options for private finance.

Private Finance

The Private Finance Initiative (PFI) was first introduced under the Conservative government in the early 1990s. From 1997, under the Labour government, PFI is subject to a major review and is now being viewed as a Public Private Partnership (PPP).

The aim of PFI/PPP is to attract private sector money to fund public sector projects for which the private sector will attract an income stream. The emphasis to date in the NHS has been on large capital schemes, for example new hospitals but the NHS has encountered significant difficulties in bringing them to a conclusion mainly because of concerns around the powers of NHS Trusts to enter into such schemes and the long-term future prospects in a rapidly changing environment such as the NHS.

A number of smaller schemes have been successful, for example retail developments on hospital sites, car parking, catering.

Leasing/Facilities Management

An alternative to outright purchase particularly of equipment and information technology is to look at some form of facilities management. This generally seeks to avoid paying out large one-off sums of capital by spreading the cost of a project over several years. Such a scheme must demonstrate value for money and certain financial criteria must be met, for example the Trust or PCT must ensure that it has an annual revenue stream to meet the cost of the lease which is likely to be an operating lease.

Facilities management may go one step further in that in addition to spreading the cost of equipment over a period of time, a private company may also take over the running of a particular function of the Trust, for example the information technology department or laundry services.

Further Reading

Department of Health (1996) *Capital Allocation – Summary Paper*, DoH, London.
Health Literature Line 0800 555 777

5

The Planning and Control of Revenue Expenditure

In the corridors of Westminster, the government's annual budget attracts a lot of press and media attention, culminating in the annual event when members of Parliament crowd into the Chamber of the House of Commons to hear the Chancellor's statement. This is usually televised, with comments from observers on the general economic climate and the measures proposed by the Chancellor to reshape or reframe the economy during the next 12 months. The process which the government of the day goes through is one of review of existing activities, and of negotiation, in following through the proposals of spending departments and agreeing in total a funding package to allow departments to carry out their objectives.

In terms of centrally organised activities, the government has aims and responsibilities, conferred by statute, and these general aims, such as the 'defence of the realm', the 'education of children of compulsory school age' or the 'maintenance of a system of health provision for all ages, irrespective of income or means' are then divided up into specific responsibilities and expressed as objectives, which are taken on board or absorbed within the objectives of a provider of that service, to the extent that the provider can fund, finance or pay for the provision of that care.

Just as central government has to plan ahead, so too have agencies and deliverers of service in the public and the private sector. The public sector has a long tradition and background of budgeting methods; originally, the amount of taxation which was made available to the public sector to carry out its functions was limited, and central government has to 'ration' the amount of cash being released to spenders. This process of rationing or of sharing out the available funds between different competing services was known as 'resource allocation'. In the health service, there was a Resource Allocation Working Party which was made up of senior officials, and they examined a whole series of indicators of the state of health of the nation, and related this to statistical and census information, in such a way that the available money nationally was redistributed by the Department of Health in fairness to known conditions within the population. At the end of this annual exercise, a finance office or director of finance would have an indication of how much money was being made available on which to run the local services for the next 12 months.

Thus, a revenue allocation is a cash-limited sum at Trust or PCT level for on-going expenditure. 'Cash limited' means that it represents a ceiling; extra funding is not likely to be available after the notification has been made, so Trusts or PCTs are obliged to keep within their notified figure of resources other than specific in-year allocations.

The annual settlement or determination of the funds for revenue purposes therefore represents an important constraint. Trusts or PCTs have to go through an annual planning exercise, in the same manner as the central government, to ensure that their policy aims, translated into objectives and into programmes will be achievable within the levels of finance which have been authorised or agreed in advance.

There are a number of ways in which revenue funds can be controlled, and different methods have been used from time to time. The main styles or methods of control are now described.

Incrementalism

Widely used, this consists of taking last year's budgeted spending, and increasing it by an across-the-board percentage of extra funds, and allowing everything to proceed into a new year without a major review. In essence, those organisations which opt for an incremental approach are doing so because they believe that the great bulk of their work is continuous or on-going from year to year, and that a percentage increase of funding to cope with the known effects of pay awards and price increases will achieve the same level of service in a future year. If you operate on an incremental basis, then the mathematics is fairly simple: you know the current year's level of costs, and you can assume that there will be a percentage increase added on for next year. The extra money may be at a different rate for pay items, for example a nurses' pay award at a certain percentage rate, than for non-pay items, such as drugs, consumable items, furniture, equipment, and so on. But is a percentage approach fair? What happens if next year's allowance is not sufficient to cover the actual costs encountered in that year?

Suppose each year you are funded to buy four new beds on a large ward, to replace ones which are no longer suitable. Suppose the basic budget is £800 per bed, plus an allowance for price rises of 5 per cent, giving £840 per bed as the amount available. If the price from the manufacturer is £880 each, the manufacturer's price increase of 10 per cent per bed has not been matched by the hospital's allowance for inflation, which was 5 per cent. The dilemma then is do you buy three beds, and keep within budget, or do you place an order for four beds, and in doing so, exceed your budget allowance, and overspend? Overspending is generally taken as an indication of poor management. If you underspend and only buy three, you could also be accused of poor management, as the ward would have had four beds out of service, and replacements available for only three.

Consequently, incrementalism may be fine in allocating out extra money, as a means of distributing resources, but it may cause problems of under- and overspending. It needs to be refined, and there are various methods of doing this.

Line–item Budgeting

This is an approach which groups together a range of similar items and controls the total spending of the heading, that is the line in the budget, instead of controlling the components one by one. For example, in the case of the four beds used earlier, the budget may include them in a heading such as 'ward equipment renewals', and as long as the total for ward equipment was not exceeded over a period of a year, the budget holder could still have four beds, even at an inflated price, if other items which were not such a priority were held back, and the money for them was not spent. Thus an overspending of £160 on the purchase of four beds would not be reported or conspicuous because somewhere in the same year a similar amount could be saved by not spending on an item which was within the same budget heading. A budget holder needs to be aware of the total value of the budget and ensure that the maximum allowed is not exceeded. This is good housekeeping in practice.

Virement

This is a French word meaning a 'transfer of money' from one heading to another. In the public sector virement is an indication that money has been switched, and although extra money has been spent, the effect overall is that the total budget has not been exceeded. The word is used when, for example, delays may have occurred which prevent money being spent, and that money is switched, or vired, to another heading, which can then go ahead and buy at a faster rate than originally planned. In total, within the confines of a year, the global previously 'approved' total is not exceeded.

Example of Virement
A PCT is planning to buy a vehicle for taking a mobile display to schools to show children the effects of neglecting their teeth, and the consequences of poor diet. The original budget is shown in Table 5.1.

Table 5.1 Dental education: original budget

Dental education in schools initiative

	£
Driver's wages and National Insurance	18,200
Publicity and promotional material	9,900
Vehicle running expenses	
Petrol, oil and servicing	750
Licensing	130
Total	**28,980**

Let us suppose that the vehicle was a four-wheel drive specialised one, and that there was a six-month waiting period between order and delivery.

If it was ordered on 1 April, the start of the financial year, the earliest it would be ready would be 1 October. There would, therefore, be no point in employing a driver until 1 October at the earliest.

So the manager in charge of health education in schools could apply for 'virement'. This releases money voted or authorised for one purpose, and transfers it to another heading, with the overall result that work of a different type is undertaken, and financially the organisation is not overspending. In this example, the manager could use the non-availability of the vehicle to move further ahead on a different type of promotion, for example to move money from the 'employees' heading of 'driver's wages and National Insurance' and transfer it to 'publicity and promotional material'. A short report would have to be drawn up to describe the circumstances of the request for virement, and to identify the proposed new expenditure.

Table 5.2　Dental education. budget report

Example of report

The original budget was prepared on the basis that the initiative for dental education was to run for a full year. Due to delays between the ordering and delivery of the vehicle, the original budget will not be needed in full, and it is proposed to bring forward a different programme, to promote healthy eating among children of primary school age, using the expenditure which was originally provided in the Schools Initiative. A display of materials relating to the new programme of Healthy Eating will be on display at the meeting of the Management Board.

Dental education in schools initiative

	Original budget	Now proposed	Amount of change
	£	£	£
Driver's wages and National Insurance	18,200	9,100	−9,100
Publicity and promotional material	9,900	19,410	+9,510
Vehicle running expenses			
Petrol, oil and servicing	750	375	−375
Licensing and Insurance	130	95	−35
Totals	**28,980**	**28,980**	**nil**

In this example, six months' spending on wages and related costs, and on petrol and licensing, has been saved by the vehicle not being available, and the manager or budget holder is putting forward a request for the money saved to be transferred to another heading, with the overall result that the total spending will not exceed the amount previously approved. This is virement, and usually applications like this are given the go-ahead providing that:

1. The saving is fortuitous, that is, it came about by conditions outside the authority's control, and was not planned to be like this. If it is a genuine saving, then it is not a back door method of paying for expenditure which was not likely to succeed in any other way.
2. The 'new' expenditure proposal is not likely to pre-empt future resources, for example an authority or a Trust would not normally approve spending on staff-related matters, as additional staff voted or approved through virement could in effect be a continuing commitment beyond the end of the period in which the fortuitous saving was made. That would have an inflationary effect, as it would be extra, continuing expenditure in the future.

Supplementary Votes or Supplementary Expenditure

The system of supplementary approvals of expenditure is used in conjunction with incremental budgeting. This allows an authority to grant an increase to a budget heading at a later date to the main budget approval, and usually as a result of extra funding becoming available. It differs from virement, as in virement no new levels of expenditure are envisaged, whereas in a supplementary situation, there is a clear acknowledgement that extra spending is being authorised.

Advantages and Disadvantages of Incrementalism

Looking at things from a total point of view, an incremental approach to budgeting has its adherents. In its favour, you can say that if last year's money was adequate to run a service, then a new approval of 'last year's money + a percentage for inflation and growth' should be a fairly easily understandable way of sharing out resources. You then concentrate each year on deciding what is an adequate measure for 'inflation', that is pay and price increases, and what is fair in total terms for 'growth', or 'new' service. However, there will be many competing claims for new 'growth' money: how does the manager handle the selection procedure, and the 'weeding out' of unsuitable bids? One way is to consider the new money in isolation: to regard it as a fund out of which new activities will be paid, and consider them as 'authority-supported initiatives' rather than departmental initiatives. If the total new money is restricted, then it makes more sense to prioritise and attach the money to those schemes which have a high profile and a high degree of support. As a consequence, some departments may receive extra funding which is disproportionately high compared with what they would have been entitled to if the available new growth money was allocated or shared out on the basis of a percentage of existing expenditure.

Thus, incrementalism focuses attention on the margins. It takes as uncontroversial the broad mass of expenditure, and primarily concentrates decision-makers' attention upon marginal changes. In doing so, we have to consider equality, fairness, equity, and future burdens on the service. Expansion of a service through extra revenue money is bound to be a contentious issue; managers who feel they have had their claims or 'bids' rejected will feel demotivated. To counter this, the trend in recent years has been to supplement the 'new money' fund by taking money from elsewhere to supplement the amounts available for expansion. For example, the principle of 'top slicing' is now fairly commonplace. This 'creams off' some of the money for ordinary revenue purposes, and adds it to the new money, so that some of the priority schemes can go ahead sooner than if they waited their turn and were totally reliant on new money only. With top slicing you are effectively taking money out of the existing revenue budget, and transferring it to the 'new growth' total. If the ordinary revenue funds are reduced in this way, there will be less money available to do the same volume of work, and health service managers are acquainted with this practice, and with the terminology which accompanies it, that of making 'efficiency savings'.

So with incrementalism: there are strong supporters of it, on the grounds that it runs from year to year without major disturbance, and is relatively consistent in its operation. Others may feel that it is too vague when coming down to a unit or ward level, and the way it operates, using percentage increases, is not sufficiently precise for day-to-day control of departmental or clinical specialty budgets. The broad majority of Trusts or PCTs operate an incremental system, and safeguard against deficiencies in the system through a range of measures:

1. A set of standing financial instructions or financial regulations define the framework within which budget holders and the authority or Trust will operate.
2. Annual budgets are analysed into convenient shorter periods, so that spending against budget can be monitored before over-spending becomes an issue.
3. Other controls are inserted, which reinforce the ability of the budget to become a useful control and feedback mechanism, for example staff numbers and staff availability is monitored through personnel departments and by operational staff, such as directors of nursing services. Not only is the cost of staff a consideration in keeping within budget, but staff mix or skill mix are equally important at ward level.
4. Computer software and systems support is needed to translate budgets which have been compiled on an incremental basis into workable and controllable management units. Ideally, budgets should cascade down an organisation so that the sum of the parts equals the total budget. Clearly, there are difficulties in sharing out some costs, especially those relating to central departments, but providing the treatment is consistent between years, and providing there is a willingness to operate as close to the budget as possible, then the budget can be a useful tool to a manager who wishes to either expand or maintain the service, as figures produced from previous periods will support the case made for expansion or extensions of service.

Zero-based Budgeting

This is an approach which is different again from incrementalism. It is an attempt to set up a forecast of what will be needed to run a service or a department, where everything is considered in detail from a starting point of having to justify every item of expenditure. It is known by its initials, ZBB. Clearly, the amount of time and effort required makes it impracticable for widespread application, for example, it would take years of work to transfer an organisation which had been running on incremental lines to a zero base. However, the technique and the procedures of zero-based budgeting are especially suitable for new situations, and managers are often forced to take a service and establish a budget for the first time. The main advantages of building a budget in this way are that it avoids the perpetuation of 'obsolete' expenditure, and it makes available a record of decisions taken and the reasons for them.

This should improve the quality of decision taking, and will monitor situations as they develop. Unexpected events which happen in the course of an operational situation will be highlighted, and after discussion, can be incorporated into the future budget planning. Zero-based budgets are therefore responsive to developments, and are less rigid than an incremental approach.

Most authorities and Trusts operate incremental budgeting on the vast majority of their activities, on the grounds that this technique mirrors national conditions and can be refined according to national pronouncements or changes in funding. They may also use a zero-based approach to a more limited extent where new proposals are coming on-stream for the first time, and the outcome of zero-based budgeting is that a separate reporting mechanism is set up which, when it has established a stability of its own, can be incorporated into the incremental base of the whole authority or the Trust.

SELF STUDY QUESTIONS

1. How would you define a cash limit in relation to a budget?

2. How would you explain virement in the context of a health service budget?

3. Describe the main features of Incrementalism and contrast it with a zero-based approach to budgeting.

Further Reading

Allen MW and Myddleton DR (1992) *Essential Management Accounting*, 2nd edn, Prentice Hall, Hemel Hempstead.

Glynn JJ, Perrin J and Murphy MP (1994) *Accounting for Managers*, Chapman & Hall, London.

Jones R and Pendlebury M (1996) *Public Sector Accounting*, 4th edn, Pitman Publishing, London.

Mellett H, Marriott N and Harries S (1993) *Financial Management in the NHS: A Manager's Handbook*, Chapman & Hall, London.

6

Setting a Budget for the First Time

Introduction

The purpose of this section is to examine the methods of setting a budget for the first time. It represents the ideal opportunity to get it right first time as it is unlikely there will be much opportunity to revisit the budget at a later date. The approach will vary according to the scale of the scheme but the same principles will apply whether it is a small or large project.

Types of Cost

The costs likely to be incurred fall into various categories:

1. direct, indirect, overheads
2. fixed, semi-fixed, variable
3. recurrent, non-recurrent.

Direct Costs – Staffing

These are the costs which will be incurred at the point of delivery of the scheme or service. The main element in the NHS will be staffing.

The key to ensuring the correct level of finance for staffing is to ensure that the numbers, grade and skill mix are accurate. It is then relatively simple to apply the costs.

The information for determining the appropriate staffing levels can be obtained from a range of sources:

1. comparison with existing similar schemes in the organisation
2. comparison with existing similar schemes in other organisations
3. professional judgement
4. use of norms or benchmarking comparisons.

The staffing mix will need to take account of:

1. the working arrangements, for example five or seven day, 9 am–5 pm or 24 hours
2. the workflow – is it busier in the mornings or afternoons or is it constant? Are there any seasonal fluctuations, for example winter/summer variations?
3. the workload and intensity of work.

The cost will need to take account of:

● sickness/absence levels
● enhancements to working conditions, for example night duty, weekend duty.

To actually arrive at a cost, various approaches may be used:

1. Staff in the NHS are usually employed on an incremental scale, that is the salary automatically increases each year for a period of 4–5 years until staff reach the maximum of the scale. Therefore in calculating the cost should it be based on the minimum, mid-point, mean or maximum of the scale? This is illustrated as follows:

£

Scale point 1 – 15,000
Scale point 2 – 15,750
Scale point 3 – 16,300
Scale point 4 – 16,650
Scale point 5 – 17,000

Therefore:

- the minimum is £15,000
- the mid-point is £16,300
- the mean is   £16,000 (that is, the average between the minimum and maximum)
- the maximum is £17,000.

Normal practice is to use the mid-point which works on the principle that there will be a reasonable turnover of staff and at any time some will be on the minimum and some on the maximum. However, the labour market has in the last few years tended to be reasonably static and it may be more prudent to cost everything at the maximum.

2. To the basic salary costs will need to be added the costs of employment or 'on-costs'. These are employers' National Insurance and employers' superannuation or pension contributions. There is no addition for employees' contributions as these are included in the basic salary costs.

3. There are two elements of enhancements to be considered:

- When staff are on holiday or off sick the work still needs to be undertaken and replacement staff will be needed in most cases. The holidays can easily be determined, the more difficult calculation is in making an assessment of how much sickness an employee may have. The usual practice is to add a percentage uplift to the cost of the basic salary.

- The second element under the heading of enhancements involves the additional cost of staff working nights and/or weekends depending on the type of service. The cost will be derived from analysing the rota that staff are required to work. For example staff might be entitled to time and a half or double time or the basic salary.

Direct Costs – Non-staffing

Using the approaches described earlier, for example comparison with other schemes/organisations/benchmarking, a similar process will need to be followed for non-pay. The main problem with non-pay is that it is very easy to forget something, in particular where it is another department that is responsible for providing the service. A very simple process to adopt is to have a standard list of all non-pay costs and to mark those that apply to your budget.

These might be classed into:

1. those that come under your direct control
2. those that are provided by other departments.

Examples under category 1 might include:

- drugs
- dressings.

Examples under category 2 might include:

- pathology
- cleaning
- radiology
- heating.

The split very much depends on the service that is being established. The key to identifying the correct cost is to ensure that the service is clearly defined so that all concerned can calculate the costs involved.

Indirect Costs

There will also be a range of costs which will not impact directly on the budget that is being established but where the service will be expected to contribute to the overall costs of the organisation. Examples could include finance or personnel. It may be that in the final analysis these departments are able to absorb the extra work but it is important to include them at the outset. It is far easier to take costs out at the beginning than to add them in at a later date.

Another way of analysing the cost is under the heading of fixed, semi-fixed and variable. As a simple equation:

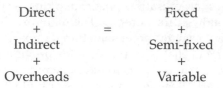

$$\begin{array}{ccc} \text{Direct} & & \text{Fixed} \\ + & & + \\ \text{Indirect} & = & \text{Semi-fixed} \\ + & & + \\ \text{Overheads} & & \text{Variable} \end{array}$$

The costs overall are the same but the treatment of the items can provide a different perspective particularly once the service is up and running.

Fixed
Fixed costs will remain unchanged irrespective of the level of service that is provided, for example whether you treat one patient or ten patients the cost is the same. Examples include rates, senior management costs.

Semi-fixed
Semi-fixed costs will change as activity changes but only at given intervals for example 1–20 patients, 20–40 patients. Other examples include staffing costs, which are particularly crucial when setting staffing levels, and cleaning arrangements.

Variable
Variable costs will change as each individual patient is treated. Examples include drugs and dressings.

Telephones provide a useful example of both a fixed and a variable cost. The rental will be fixed because irrespective of the number of calls the rental is the same. However, the call charge will be variable as it will be totally dependent on the number of calls made.

The analysis under the headings of fixed, semi-fixed and variable can be particularly important if a service is to be introduced in stages and also for monitoring purposes once the service is up and running.

Recurrent/Non-recurrent
Terminology that is often used in the NHS refers to costs (and funding) that is recurrent or non-recurrent.

Recurrent costs are those that occur year on year.

Non-recurrent are those that occur only once. These can often relate to costs incurred in the set-up of a new service.

SELF-STUDY QUESTIONS

1. Distinguish between what is meant by mid-point and mean in the context of salary scales

2. Indicate some of the on-costs which are usually associated with salaries' estimates

3. Distinguish between fixed, semi-variable and variable costs and give health service examples for each category of cost.

Further Reading

Mellett H, Marriott N and Harries S (1993) *Financial Management in the NHS: A Manager's Handbook*, Chapman & Hall, London.

7

Monitoring of Budget Performance

Introduction

The purpose of this chapter is to examine the process for monitoring budget performance and to examine cost behaviour, exception reporting and ways of dealing with under- and overspendings.

Budget Monitoring

Budget monitoring in the NHS, and indeed most organisations, takes place over a 12-month time frame with month-by-month analysis of performance. A typical budget statement will have a series of headings such as:

- annual budget
- monthly budget
- monthly expenditure
- monthly variance
- cumulative budget
- cumulative expenditure
- cumulative variance to date.

In addition there will also be information on staffing typically:

- funded establishment
- actual establishment.

The budget statement will form the basis for determining a range of issues, in particular whether there is a need to take corrective action and what form of action that will entail.

One important feature of the budget statement is that it should confirm simply what the budget holder should already know. Any variances should not come as a surprise. However, in reality the budget statement is often the first indicator that everything is either alright or that there are problems.

It is equally important to understand not only why a budget may be overspent but also why it is underspent.

Analysing the Budget

Typically a budget statement will be produced as soon as possible after the end of the month to which it refers. The aim should be no later than ten working days.

The immediate focus will be on the overall position but it will be necessary to check the movements on individual budget lines to ensure that there is nothing untoward. It is the responsibility of each budget holder to undertake this review.

Individual budget statements will be amalgamated to produce the summary position for a directorate. This will normally be accompanied by a written report from the accountant (directorate accountant/financial advisor) highlighting key points.

As mentioned earlier, it is important that underspendings are looked at just as closely as overspendings for example:

1. Has something been missed?
2. Has expenditure been incurred which relates to future months?
3. Was the budget holder expecting expenditure to be incurred? Has an assessment been made if the invoice has not been paid?

Overall the budget holders need to satisfy themselves that the position accurately reflects the position of their department.

Phasing the Budget

A common problem in the NHS is the extent to which a budget should be phased in line with anticipated expenditure. Simply to take your annual budget and divide it by 12 which does not reflect the expenditure pattern could result in incorrect decisions being taken.

Some simple examples are:

1. There is a greater volume of medical cases in the winter than the summer.
2. Energy costs will be higher in the winter than the summer.
3. Drugs are issued daily to patients. Therefore, minor changes should be made for 30- and 31-day months.
4. Bank holidays will result in higher salaries and wages costs because of enhanced payment rates.

Terminology

Terminology can sometimes be difficult to interpret. An overspending may be indicated by:

1. a + in front of the variance
2. adverse/unfavourable/bad.

An underspending may be indicated by:

1. a – in front of the variance
2. favourable/good
3. brackets ( ) around the figures.

Taking Action

Any course of action will be determined by the reason for the over- or underspending. The action itself is likely to take time to have an effect. By the time that the position has been validated as correct and appropriate analysis undertaken, three to four weeks may have elapsed.

The decision on what action to take may require senior authorisation. Also, given that the majority of expenditure in the NHS is staffing, changes to staffing levels could again take time to implement. The view has to be taken as to whether the action is permanent or temporary.

It is important, therefore, seriously to consider whether the action proposed will, in the time available, correct the budgetary position. This can be very difficult to achieve if such a situation arises late in the financial year, and may mean that additional short-term measures are required to correct any in-year issues.

If there is likely to be an underspending, it is also important to identify this early so that decisions can be taken as to whether to use the money for something else, or to leave it as an underspending to offset an overspending elsewhere in the organisation.

Further Reading

Glynn JJ, Perrin J and Murphy MP (1995) *Accounting for Managers*, Chapman & Hall, London.

Mellett H, Marriott N and Harries S (1993) *Financial Management in the NHS: A Manager's Handbook*, Chapman & Hall, London.

Wilson RMS and McHugh G (1996) *Financial Analysis: A Managerial Introduction*, Cassell, London.

8

Putting it all Together

Introduction

One of the features of the health service is that the whole activity within a hospital is geared towards keeping within budget, and that the total spending is made up of adding together all the small budgets. Understanding the organisational structure is important. This chapter outlines how the structure of the hospital is reflected in the financial information on which important decisions and switches of resources are made.

Organisational Structures

Under the Resource Management Initiative (1991), hospitals were divisionalised, and the idea which had been developed during the 1980s of adopting a specialty approach was formalised by the creation of *directorates*. Each manager of a directorate is supported by a nurse manager and a business manager. Thus, if a hospital had a specialty of, for example, ear, nose and throat (ENT), the directorate or management team of that directorate would be a consultant or doctor, as head of the directorate, a nurse manager, and a business manager. The way in which a hospital divides up its specialties into directorates will determine the organisational structure of the hospital, and the budgeting will be a natural consequence, flowing from the predetermined organisational arrangements. Organisational structure is shown in Figure 8.1.

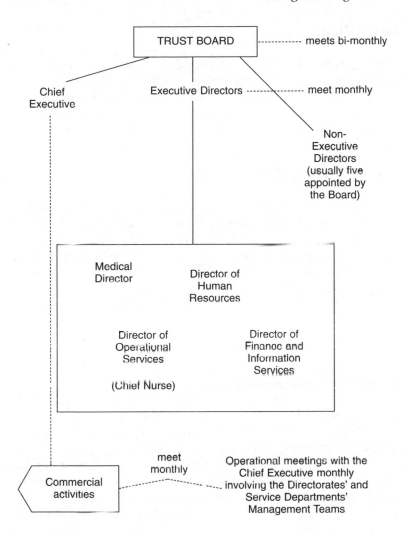

Figure 8.1 Organisational structure of a large acute hospital

The Challenge

Assuming that a hospital has divided itself into directorates, the challenge then comes of containing expenditure within the expected levels of income. The reason we have financial information is to enable managers to monitor spending and to take corrective action if preliminary indications reveal that overspending is likely.

How are Budgets Determined?

The income which a Trust receives is largely as a result of negotiated contracts, as explained in Chapter 1. The total possible or estimated income is known in advance. The task of the directorates is to prepare their own expenditure budgets in such a way that the totality of expenditure is within the income estimate. Table 8.1 shows a sample summary of income and expenditure.

Some departments have no income. Radiography acts as a support service for the rest of the hospital, and in such cases, an equitable way has to be found of sharing the cost of that department among the departments which have use of its services, so that in effect radiography has a notional income which is derived from recharges to other departments or directorates.

So the task of determining the budget starts by estimating the expected level of activity within a directorate for a future 12-month period, and calculating how much that level of activity will cost. As a starting point, one might take the approved spending plans of last year, and add on any development money which has been secured, and an allowance for levels of inflation, covering an estimate of increases in pay and prices affecting the service, and then the total expenditure estimate is the sum of three things: last year, development and inflation. Table 8.2 shows a sample ward budget.

The total costs are then linked to the level of activity, for example, to arrive at indicators of possible costs for clinical intervention (for example, costs per consultant day, costs of a particular procedure, or output such as in-patient days) and if the costs are in line with the agreed levels of funding, the directorate's budget is approved.

If there is a potential shortfall between expenditure and income, then the directorate may look to renegotiate its contracts, or seek efficiency savings to bring the expenditure closer to the level of

Table 8.1 Summary of income and expenditure for a large acute hospital

	General surgery £	General medical £	Children's services £	Obstetrics and gynaecology £	Ear, nose and throat £	Radiology £	Pathology £	Pharmacy £	Theatres £	Support services £
Income										
Block contract income										
Extra contract referrals										
Private charges										
Service increment for teaching and research										
Total income										
Direct Expenditure										
Pay (analysed by grade)										
Non-pay (subjective analysis of direct costs)										
Clinical costs										
Internal recharges for support services										
Medical services										
Radiology										
Pathology										
Non-medical services										
Cleaning										
Porters										
General										
Total expenditure										

Table 8.2 Ward budget

Budget details Whole time Staff numbers	Budget heading	2003/04 Revised budget £	Projected spend to Jan 2004 £	Actual spend to Jan 2004 £	Variance overspend (underspend) £
	Pay				
3	Ward sisters	81,000	60,750	59,000	(1,750)
8	Staff nurses	168,000	117,600	118,600	1,000
12	Assistant nurses	205,200	153,900	152,000	(1,900)
2	Clerical assistants	25,000	18,750	18,200	(550)
	National Insurance				
	Ward sisters	8,910	6,680	6,490	(190)
	Staff nurses	18,480	13,860	13,050	(810)
	Assistant nurses	22,580	16,940	16,720	(220)
	Clerical assistants	2,750	2,060	2,000	(60)
	Ward Supplies				
	Drugs and dressings	22,500	16,880	17,230	350
	Consumables	9,700	7,280	7,580	300
	Ward sundries	5,200	3,900	3,700	(200)
		569,320	**418,600**	**414,570**	**(4,030)**

income available to that directorate. This is where you have to consider the balance between emergency and non-emergency work: the clinical priorities within a department, and the differences between elective and non-elective surgery. In the same way, the introduction of a new drug may trigger off more demand for a particular type of treatment, and if you are funded according to previously lower levels of treatment, you have either to acquire more funds to treat more patients, or restrict the number of patients treated, simply because the funding is not there.

Cost Pressures

One of the terms used in the context of directorates' spending plans is that of 'cost pressures'. This can mean a number of things. One type of cost pressure is the inflationary cost of drugs: for example, some drugs are expensive to produce, and manufacturers may increase their prices in order to recover their costs, particularly if demand for the drug is falling. That is an external cost pressure, imposed from outside the hospital, by a drug manufacturer. Another cost pressure is where changes in clinical practice recommend new drugs being used in areas where there is no base budget for this kind of development. So extra spending is a cost pressure. If you imagine a budget being a fixed amount of money available for a directorate for a period of a year, a more expensive drug or a new drug may take up money in the budget at a faster rate than money was used in the past, and the effect is that in the current conditions you either have to modify your caseload to stay within budget, or keep the same level of activity and overspend. Overspending in one directorate can cause problems in another, so the collective pressure is really to stay within budget, and this means reducing activity accordingly, until more resources can be negotiated or found to restore the planned level of activity.

Devolved Management

The reason for finance being an important consideration is that it is a means of measuring the plans and objectives of directorates, within the environment of business planning and agreed objective setting at the senior decision-making level of the Trust. If information is available at directorate level, then corrective action can be taken to ensure that the whole hospital's spending is in line with its plans.

Financial information is considered both strategically for the hospital as a whole, and managerially at the level of business planning, at directorate level. The use of financial information acts both as a planning mechanism, and as a control mechanism. Putting money values on activity helps to identify how much activity is expected, and as the year passes by and money has been used up, you also have an indication of how much money is left and how much activity can be afforded in the remaining time before a new year and a new budget are in place.

9

An Introduction to Primary Care Trusts

Introduction and Function of Primary Care Trusts (PCTs)

Primary Care Trusts were established as NHS organisations under the Health Act 1999, *The NHS Plan* and *Shifting the Balance of Power*.

The functions of PCTs are set out in *Primary Care Trusts: Financial Framework*, published by the Department of Health in 2000. This states:

> The functions of PCTs are:
>
> (a) to improve the health of the community
> (b) to develop primary care
> (c) to commission hospital and community health services
> (d) to provide community health services.

The financial framework also requires PCTs to achieve three financial duties. These act as the financial environment within which PCTs carry out the above functions.

PCT Financial Duties

The three financial duties are:

1. *To keep within the PCT's cash and resource limit*
The Department of Health allocates its share of the Parliamentary vote to PCTs via a cash and resource limit. The resource limit reflects

the amount of funding which the PCT is expected to keep within when providing services for a year. The cash limit is a spending target which relates to cash expenditure, which is defined as the value of the resource limit minus the cost of capital charges and minus other forms of non-cash expenditure. PCTs must both keep within these limits and materially match them.

2. *PCTs must achieve full cost recovery for their provider functions*
This means that the expenditure in providing primary and community health care must equal the income received, that is, a position of 'breakeven'. The income will come from various sources, such as the PCT's own resource limit and Service Level Agreements (SLAs) with neighbouring PCTs and with local authorities.

3. *To achieve a 3.5 % Return on Capital Employed (ROCE)*
This target was set at 6% prior to 2003/2004.

The PCT Cash Limit and Resource Limit

As discussed earlier in this chapter the PCT has a duty to keep within its cash limit. This is different to keeping within the PCT's resource limit.

The former refers to expenditure *made* in a particular year and the latter to expenditure *relating* to a particular year. For instance, if a £150,000 payment is made by XYZ PCT in Month 1 of financial year 2000 but it is a late payment relating to Month 12 of year 1999 then the expenditure is part of 1999's resource limit but 2000's cash limit. Table 9.1 demonstrates the distinction.

Table 9.1   Cash and resource limit distinction

Payment £	Month/Year Payment Made	Month/Year Payment Relates To	Relevant Resource Limit	Relevant Cash Limit
150,000	1/2000	12/1999	1999	2000
175,000	5/2000	4/2000	2000	2000
160,000	6/2000	11/1999	1999	2000
100,000	12/2000	1/2001	2001	2000

Managing the PCT's Cash Limit

Cash management is fundamental to keeping within a PCT's cash limit. This means managing when payments are made to ensure a PCT is not left with too much cash at the end of a period or runs out of cash beforehand. Should a PCT realise it is at risk of either of these problems then four tools are available to manage the position.

If a PCT realises it is at risk of running out of cash, it can delay paying invoices and/or request payments from other organisations that either owe the PCT money or will do so in the future (a prepayment).

If a PCT realises it is at risk of having too much cash at the end of the period then it can pay its outstanding and upcoming debts (prepayments again, this time from rather than to the PCT) and ask those who owe the PCT money to delay payment as this will stop more cash entering the PCT's accounts.

Study Exercise: Year-end Cash Management

It is March 2003 and Central PCT has one more round of payments to make and collect before the financial year ends. Monitoring of the PCT's cash position shows that, if it makes and receives its usual payments it will have £1,000,000 of cash remaining in its accounts at year end. This would mean undershooting on its cash limit and so cash management techniques must be employed in order to clear the PCT's account.

Further investigation highlights the following:

1. South PCT owe Central PCT their regular monthly Service Level Agreement of £300,000.
2. North PCT have a Service Level Agreement with Central PCT of £120,000 per annum. They have paid this in full for the current year.
3. Central PCT still owe East PCT £80,000 relating to the previous year.
4. Central PCT usually pay the local council £630,000 in Month 1 of each financial year.

Task: Use any combination of these four pieces of financial information to manage Central PCT's cash position.

Solution: There are various combinations of prepayments, payments and requesting payment delays from the four pieces of information that will bring the Central PCT cash position to nil. The suggested solution in Table 9.2 is only one of these.

Table 9.2   Central PCT year-end cash position

	Performance against Cash Limit (£)
Initial forecast assuming usual monthly payments and receipts	−1,000,000
Prepay local council annual sum	+630,000
Request South PCT delay paying regular monthly sum	+300,000
Pay outstanding East PCT debt	+80,000
Request prepayment of one month of North PCT Service Level Agreement	−10,000
Year-end cash position	**0**

Through a combination of prepayments made and received and delays to regular payments, Central PCT has managed its cash position to zero. This means it has managed its cash limit for the year.

This solution is very simplistic as it assumes all other parties involved are able to go along with Central PCT's plans. For instance, if South PCT is forecast to overshoot their cash limit by £300,000 they will be more than happy to delay their monthly payment. However, if South PCT plans on making the payment in order to balance their cash position then this avenue will not be open to Central PCT.

The most effective way of managing the annual cash limit is to manage the position monthly. The techniques are the same as shown in the above exercise for the year end. The Department of Health encourages monthly management by asking PCTs to 'draw down' cash from the NHS Bank (the part of the Paymaster General's Office relating to health care) in advance of the month ahead and then monitoring PCTs against this. PCTs must therefore forecast their monthly needs in advance, and either having cash remaining at month end or requesting more cash within the month highlights a failure to keep to this forecast.

Achieving Full Cost Recovery for Provider Functions

A PCT may provide a series of services to both its own population and the population of other PCTs and organisations. The requirement to achieve full cost recovery for these services therefore requires robust Service Level Agreements to be in place and management of the various income streams. A PCT's provider functions may therefore look like those shown in Table 9.3

Table 9.3 Management of income streams to ensure full cost recovery for provider functions

XYZ PCT Provider Function	Total Expenditure	Income Streams			Total Income
		XYZ PCT Resource Limit	SLA with ABC PCT	SLA with Local Authority	
District Nursing	£1.5m	£0.9m	£0.6m		£1.5m
Health Visiting	£1.5m	£1.1m	£0.4m		£1.5m
Dental Services	£0.8m	£0.8m	-	-	£0.8m
Speech Therapy	£1.2m	£0.6m	£0.3m	£0.3m	£1.2m
Learning Difficulties	£2.8m	£1.1m	£1.0m	£0.7m	£2.8m
Total Provider Function	**£7.8m**	£4.5m	£2.3m	£1.0m	**£7.8m**

Relationships with Other Organisations

NHS Trusts

PCTs commission the expected level of services from mental health and acute Trusts for their resident populations. Mental health, ambulance and acute Trusts negotiate and agree, through their SLAs, the level of service for a level of income with each PCT they provide services to. Due to the size and nature of PCT provider services, these may be provided from mental health, ambulance, or acute Trust sites. Consequently, the PCT may have to purchase non-health services, such as cleaning or maintenance from the Trusts as it would be inefficient to provide its own support, or to duplicate aspects of work which were already there. Such costs, in support of PCT provision, are known as 'recharges', meaning a recharge of costs from the mental health, ambulance, or acute hospital Trust to the PCT.

Also, in the interests of value for money, PCTs may purchase services such as their payroll function, or the manpower and systems for paying invoices, from the larger Trust departments, rather than run their own service. These are known as 'shared service centres' and again, involve recharges to the PCT.

Strategic Health Authorities (StHAs)

StHAs are responsible for measuring performance in PCTs. This is known as 'performance monitoring'. As a consequence, PCT finance departments send regular reports and returns to the StHA. These reports and returns detail the PCT's latest financial position. For example, the report at the end of June will show the end of Quarter 1 (April to June) income and expenditure position and forecast for the end of year, based on the first quarter's actual expenditure, and estimates for the remaining three periods of three months (Quarters 2,3, and 4) covering in total nine months of the financial year. The reports and returns will include more information than just financial performance, and may include data about activity levels or performance statistics against a target 'take-up' level for a screening programme.

Department of Health (DoH)

The DoH allocates its financial resources directly to PCTs. In addition, the performance information which the StHAs collect from PCTs in their area is amalgamated and passed to the DoH to provide a national set of information. The DoH also manages national collections of information: for example, each year PCTs carry out Reference Cost analysis for the DoH. These costs compare costs for providing services across all PCTs and show where individual PCTs are more, or less, efficient than others. The importance of Reference Costs is growing, for example, it is envisaged that Trusts will ultimately only be able to charge an average of Reference Cost price for its services. This will act as an incentive to make services more efficient where the Trust appears to be comparatively expensive in comparison to other Trusts, and will cause a downward pressure on costs.

Local Authorities (LAs)

LAs and PCTs work closely together in various areas. The relationship has developed to the extent that the processes known as 'Joint Working', 'Partnership Development' and/or 'Pooled Budgets' exist between many LAs and PCTs. There are areas of community health services which work closely with staff in local authorities, such as in providing services for adults with learning difficulties, where the NHS, Social Services and education departments are all concerned in the management of an on-going situation. As a result, many PCTs and LAs have developed partnerships for both learning difficulties provision and commissioning, in which both organisations 'pool' their money, manpower, and management to provide and fund the service collectively from one department.

Outside these arrangements, PCTs commission from and provide services to LAs, such as placements in residential homes or beds on palliative care wards.

General Practitioners (GPs)

PCTs support the services provided by general practitioners in a number of ways including funding certain areas of their work, offering support staff to practices under pressure and commissioning entire GP services from practices that have opted to join the personal medical services (PMS) system. The new GP contract also develops the relationship between PCTs and non-PMS practices and is discussed in Chapter 10.

Other Non-NHS Organisations

PCTs commission services from non-NHS organisations, such as nursing homes and the voluntary sector. These can range from the long-term provision of a residential placement to a person with on-going mental health problems or the funding of a one-off project to encourage children to eat fruit every day.

Other PCTs

The financial and service relationship between local PCTs can be complex. As with LAs, there exist areas of mutual interest and this can lead to what is known as 'Joint Working'. In many cases, neighbouring PCTs will commission services from the same providers and the actions and projects of one PCT will often affect and include its neighbours. To this end, many PCTs have entered into 'Lead Commissioning Agreements'. This means that in negotiations with some providers, the finance team of one PCT will represent its neighbour PCT as well. There also exists a provision relationship between local PCTs. For example, it may be more efficient for a single PCT not to provide its own learning difficulties or chiropody service to its own population. In such situations, a PCT may provide the service to its neighbours by drawing up and consenting to a Service Level Agreement which is between two (or more) PCTs.

PCT Standing Orders and Standing Financial Instructions

All PCTs are required to have standing orders and standing financial instructions. These set out the financial responsibilities of the PCT and how they affect the work of all staff. An example of a summary of a set of standing orders and financial instructions is shown in Tables 9.4 and 9.5.

Table 9.4 Example of a staff guide to a set of standing orders for a Primary Care Trust

---

Editor's note:
A set of standing orders will be issued by a Chief Executive of a PCT and from time to time, based on experience, extra clauses may be added, or financial limits within them may be changed, in the light of circumstances and economic conditions. What follows is a staff guide to a set of standing orders.

The standing orders are usually summarised in the form of a leaflet, which is issued to all staff. The leaflet summarises the responsibilities of staff working for the PCT, and incorporates the requirements of law and government policy.

Staff have a duty to acquaint themselves with standing orders, to know where they are kept, and to observe them in relation to every aspect of their job, and to report any deviation from the observance of standing orders to their line manager, and ultimately to the senior management of the PCT.

The XYZ Primary Care Trust

The PCT must have:
  A Chairperson
  5 Non-officer members

5 Officer members including:
- Chief Executive
- Director of Finance
- Chair of the Executive Committee
- 2 persons appointed by the Chair of the PCT following their nomination by the Executive Committee.

The standing orders will give information relating to the rules for the appointment of the Chair, Vice-Chair and Directors of the PCT.

Meetings of the PCT

The standing orders will explain the requirements for meetings of the PCT Board and the rules concerning the notification of such meetings.

Delegation

These give the Board the power to delegate its functions. The PCT Board must approve a scheme of delegation. This sets out delegated responsibilities and financial limits for the authorisation of expenditure.

Committees

The Trust will have three main committees Executive, Audit and Remuneration. In addition there is a Risk Committee and a Clinical Governance Committee.

Declaration and Register of Interests

Board and Executive Committee members must declare any interests that are relevant and material to the PCT Board.

The Chief Executive will ensure that a register of such interests is maintained.

Disqualification of Members with an Interest

Members who declare a pecuniary interest will be disqualified from taking part in certain discussions and decision-making processes.

Standards of Business Conduct

If a member of staff, or their partner, has an interest in a business that is proposing to enter into a contract with the PCT, then that officer must notify the Chief Executive in writing.

Staff should also declare to the Chief Executive any other employment or business that may conflict with the interests of the PCT

Candidates for appointment must declare relationships to a director or other officer of the PCT.

Directors or officers of the PCT must disclose any relationships to a candidate.

Tendering and Contract Procedure

This section in the standing orders details the rules for the contracting of goods and services, and who may enter into contracts on behalf of the PCT.

Rules in tendering and obtaining quotations can also be found here. A summary is included in this leaflet. Specific instructions exist should a competitive tendering exercise be undertaken for services currently provided in-house.

Health Care Service Agreements

Service agreements with NHS providers for the supply of health care services shall be drawn up in accordance with the NHS and Community Care Act 1990, and administered by the PCT.

Disposal of Assets

Rules on competitive tendering and quotation procedures on the disposal of an asset are shown in this section of the standing orders. No assets can be disposed of without appropriate sanction.

Custody of the Seal and Procedures for Signing and Sealing Documents

Each PCT will have a seal with which to imprint its name into deeds and other legal documents. The Chief Executive or officers nominated by the Board may sign agreements. Where signing a document is a stage in legal proceedings, then the signature of the Chief Executive is required.

Miscellaneous

The Chief Executive is responsible for ensuring that all directors and staff are notified and understand their responsibilities within the standing orders. The standing financial instructions and scheme of delegation shall have the effect as if incorporated into the standing orders. The standing orders will be reviewed annually.

Guide to the Delegated Financial Limits

Only those people with delegated budgets and or authority under the scheme of delegation may legitimately incur expenditure on behalf of the PCT, and then only in relation to the budgets they hold. Budgets may NOT be exceeded.

Unless otherwise notified by the Chief Executive or Director of Finance the delegated authorisation limits for managers are set out here and may not be exceeded.

Service Level Agreements with health care organisations for the provision of health care or shared services fall outside of this guidance.

The requisitioning of goods and services may be authorised as follows unless express written authorisation is give extending these limits:

Up to £5,000	Budget Manager
Up to £25,000	Director
Over £25,000	Chief Executive or Director of Finance
Over £50,000	Two of either the Chief Executive or the Director of Finance – and reported to the Board
Over £100,000	Board approval required

Contracts for goods and services exceeding 12 months:

These must all be authorised by a director.

Tendering Limits

There are no formal quotation or tendering procedures relating to expenditure below £1,000. There is a duty upon those responsible for the expenditure to achieve the best value for money.

There is a requirement to obtain a minimum of two written quotations on all goods and services costing between £1,000 and £9,999, and a minimum of three written quotations between £10,000 and £29,999. Waivers may be granted in specific circumstances.

The formal tendering process applies to all expenditure over £30,000 and must be adhered to unless the expenditure fits the criteria under which formal tendering may be waived.

The lowest quotation should be accepted. A quote other than the lowest may be accepted with the approval of the Chief Executive or the Director of Finance.

Table 9.5 Example of a staff guide to a set of standing financial instructions for a Primary Care Trust

---

Editor's Note:

A set of standing financial instructions will be issued by a Chief Executive of a PCT in conjuction with the Director of Finance.

These instructions are a method of setting out rules which will apply across the whole of the PCT so that in certain routine processes, such as the appointment of staff, or the payment of creditors, common rules are used by every section and department.

The standing financial instructions will exist either as a web-page on the PCT's intranet, or in a loose-leaf printed format. All sections dealing with financial processing will have a printed copy.

A shortened version, in the form of a leaflet, is set out below, and is issued to all staff. The leaflet summarises the responsibilities of staff working for the PCT, and incorporates the requirements of law and government policy.

Staff have a duty to acquaint themselves with standing financial instructions, to know where they are kept, or how they can be accessed, and to observe them in relation to every aspect of their job, and to report any deviation from the observance of standing financial instructions to their line manager, and ultimately to the senior management of the PCT.

Responsibilities and Delegation

The Chief Executive has overall executive responsibility for the PCT's activities and is responsible to the Chair and Board.

The Director of Finance is responsible for:

● Implementation and monitoring of PCT Financial Policies.
● Maintaining an effective system of financial control.
● Retention of records to support the financial position of the PCT.

All Board and Executive Committee members and employees are responsible for:

- Security of all PCT property.
- Avoiding loss.
- Being cost effective in the use of resources.
- Adhering to the requirements of standing orders and standing financial instructions.

Audit

The Board has established an Audit Committee to provide an independent and objective view of internal controls.

Internal audit will review, appraise and report on the adequacy and completeness of financial and other management related controls.

External auditors are appointed by the Audit Commission. They have a statutory role, reviewing the PCT's annual accounts and also perform value-for-money studies.

Cash Limits

The PCT may not exceed its cash limit, and may only draw down cash at the time of need.

Planning

The Chief Executive will prepare an annual plan for submission to and approval by the Board.

The Director of Finance will:

- Submit an annual budget to the Board for approval.
- Provide the Board with monthly reports showing the PCT's financial position.

Budgetary Delegation

Budget holders must not exceed the budgetary limits set by the Board. Any budgeted funds not required for their original purpose revert to the control of the Chief Executive.

Banking Procedures

The Director of Finance has responsibility for managing the PCT's banking arrangements.

No other banking arrangements may be entered into on the PCT's behalf.

Income

The Director of Finance is responsible for the collection, banking and recording of all monies due to the PCT.

All income due to the PCT must be notified to the Director of Finance.

Security of Cash and Cheques

- The Director of Finance must agree all forms and systems for recording cash transactions.
- Suitable facilities will be provided for the collection and holding of cash.
- Encashment of private cheques using official money is prohibited.

- All cash and cheques must be banked intact.
- Unofficial funds should not be held without a written indemnity absolving the PCT of responsibility.

Remuneration and Staff Appointments

The Board established a Remuneration Committee to advise on the salary and terms of service for the Chief Executive and other Executive officers.

Board approval is required for proposals regarding the pay and terms for all staff.

Appointment of Staff

No member of the Executive Committee or member of staff may engage, re-engage or regrade employees on either a permanent or a temporary basis, or hire agency staff or agree changes in any aspect of remuneration unless authorised to do so by the Chief Executive.

Payroll Processing

Responsibility for procedures and policies lies with the Director of Finance.

Delegated responsibility lies with nominated managers for ensuring time records and other notifications are completed on a timely basis.

Non-pay Expenditure

- Expenditure must not exceed budget.
- Value for money should be ensured when items are requisitioned.
- Prepayments are only permitted in exceptional circumstances.
- Official orders should be used for the purchase of all goods and services.
- Thresholds are set out in the Standing Orders detailing the limits at which tenders or written quotations are required. Orders must not be completed in such a way as to avoid these thresholds.
- Orders should not be issued to a firm that has made offers of gifts.
- Goods on loan or trial should not be accepted if it may tie the PCT to future purchases.
- Petty cash purchases are restricted in type and to a maximum of £25 per voucher.

Capital Programme

The Chief Executive will ensure there is an appraisal and approval system in place for determining priorities.

Asset Register

An asset register will be maintained and reviewed on a regular basis.

Stores

Minimum stock will be held to support the on-going work of the PCT. Stocktakes will be performed on an annual basis.

Disposals

Before disposing of any PCT asset, the head of department must inform the Director of Finance of the value of the item.

Losses and Special Payments

- If an employee suspects or discovers a loss, then the head of department should be informed, who will inform the Chief Executive.
- If a criminal offence is suspected, the police will be notified.
- A losses and compensation register will be maintained.

Information Technology

The PCT will ensure that it has adequate security in place for its data, hardware and software.

Patients' Property

The PCT will provide safe custody for patients' money or other personal property handed in by patients.

Risk Management

The Chief Executive will ensure there are appropriate systems for risk management within the PCT.

Further Guidance

Further guidance on compliance with the standing financial instructions can be obtained from the PCT Director of Finance.

SELF-STUDY QUESTIONS

1. What are the financial duties of Primary Care Trusts?

2. What are the functions of Primary Care Trusts?

3. In what ways will an acute hospital Trust be involved with a Primary Care Trust, and what types of agreements and financial arrangements will need to be in place to identify and measure the extent of their working arrangements?

Further Reading

Department of Health (2000) *Primary Care Trusts: Financial Framework*, DoH, London.

Department of Health (2000) *The NHS Plan*, DoH, London.

Department of Health (2001) *Modernising the NHS: Shifting the Balance of Power*, DoH, London.

10

The Dual Role of Primary Care Trusts

The Primary Care Trust as Commissioner

As Chapter 9 explained, one of the four functions of PCTs is *to commission hospital and community health services.*

PCTs are the predominant commissioners of health care for their resident population. The first part of this chapter examines the various mechanisms in place that support and enable effective PCT commissioning, how PCTs commission, and from whom.

The Commissioning Cycle

The Three-year Plan (Prepared During the September–December Period)

At the outset of the arrangements for PCTs, the commissioning cycle began with an annual plan being drawn up. However, from April 2003 this position changed and PCTs now commission services from providers over a three-year period. The intention of this change is to give both commissioners and providers more stability and continuity in their financial and health care planning and to help better long term strategic decision making.

The DoH allocates financial resources to PCTs for a three-year period and PCTs then translate these resources, in negotiation with providers, into health care services. In order to do this, NHS managers and health care professionals take into account historic activity, expected future needs, and government and local plans for service improvement and expansion. All of this must fit within the overall financial resources available.

Source and Application of Funds – SAPP – Prepared During the Period December to March

The SAPP matches the source (income or resource) of funds available to a PCT with the application (expenditure) of these funds. This acts as a summary demonstration of the balance required between spending and funding received. Table 10.1 shows a simplified outline of a SAPP schedule.

Table 10.1 Source and application of funds 2003/2004

XYZ Primary Care Trust	£000's
1. Source of funds	
2002/2003:	
DoH allocation	95,000
Income from other PCTs	4,000
Income from local authorities	1,000
Sub-total (2002/2003 baseline)	100,000
2003/2004:	
Notified growth in DoH allocation (10%)	9,500
Negotiated growth in other income	500
Total source of funds (2003/2004 baseline)	110,000
2. Application of funds	
2002/2003:	
Services to resident population (2002/2003 baseline)	100,000
2003/2004:	
Generic cost pressures	5,000
New service developments	5,000
Total application of funds (2003/2004 baseline)	**110,000**

Service and Financial Framework – SAFF – Prepared in the Period January to March

The SAFF is a detailed representation of how the application of funds translates into activity or services, and the element of finances identified to support that activity. Within the SAFF model, the financial support for the current level of service is identified. In addition, the model identifies how the developments in the service, such as ensuring the achievement of government waiting list targets or access to a primary care professional, are represented in terms of both service and funding.

In practice, a first draft, three-year version of the SAPP and the SAFF may be used as the models for the three-year plan.

Local Delivery Plan – LDP – Prepared in the Period March to May

The LDP (also known as the Annual Delivery Plan or Agreement) is a narrative document that sets out how a PCT is to achieve that year's targets by departments or by directorates. It is produced in the early months of the financial year and typically will identify the various targets relevant to a directorate, such as reducing waiting time from a patient's first visit to a GP, through referral and diagnosis to being treated by a hospital specialist from a directorate of primary care. It will then detail how the directorate will work towards achievement of that target and who will be responsible for each step. The role of the PCT finance function within this will be to support the directorate in achieving each step, first by identifying the necessary funds and second by helping to ensure that the process remains within the level of funds identified.

Franchise Plan – Prepared in the Months of February to March

In 2002/2003, the Franchise Plan was introduced. Each Strategic Health Authority is charged with producing a Franchise Plan for its health sector, showing how the various plans of the Authority's PCTs will meet the requirements laid down by the DoH, including the various government targets set. The Franchise Plan includes a collation of the PCT SAFF's for the area.

Commissioning Cycle Summary

The plans which begin with frontline staff discussing with managers their needs for a new year, progress through the PCT finance function and are incorporated into SAFFs and SAPPs, and then are sent to the DoH as part of each Strategic Health Authority's Franchise Plan. There are numerous other models to assist a PCT in commissioning effectively. However the main ones are those which have been already discussed in this chapter. Table 10.2 outlines the annual process in the commissioning cycle.

Table 10.2 Commissioning cycle summary

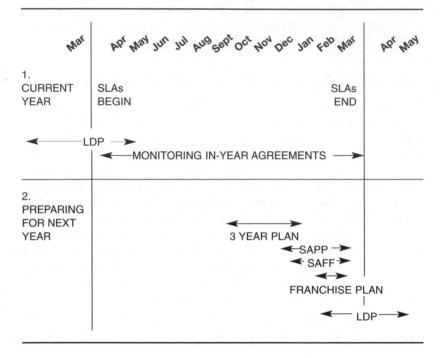

Balancing Resources and Targets

A fundamental requirement in the effective management of PCTs is the balance between maintaining the current level of health care provision, moving towards and reaching the new targets which the NHS is given each year, and keeping within the financial resources made available.

In a typical commissioning cycle, the financial pressures for a new year will initially exceed the level of resource available. The PCT then has to find ways to manage the issue. Table 10.3 gives an example.

As a result of this gap, various decisions are required. The first of these is what, up to the available £900,000, is funded of the pressures against remaining growth.

The second is if and how the size of the £1,400,000 gap can be reduced and/or the £900,000 available can be made to go further. For example:

Table 10.3 New year financial pressures

	£000's
Growth in PCT resource (additional income)	10,000
Generic cost pressures: Pay	5,000
Non-pay	1,000
Government targets	2,000
DoH top-slices (e.g. Clinical Negligence Insurance)	500
NICE recommendations	600
Sub-total	9,100
Remaining growth available	900
Pressures against remaining growth:	
Activity increases	800
Service developments	1,400
Full year effect of previous year's investments	400
Cash releasing efficiency saving (CRES)	(300)
Total pressures against remaining growth	2,300
Remaining growth available	(900)
Financial pressures funding gap	1,400

- Is it possible to meet the government's targets for less expenditure?
- Can any of the service developments be carried out for less spending, or can they be delayed until later in the year, or even until next year?
- Are efficiency savings, over and above the currently planned £300,000, possible?
- Are non-financial solutions, such as changes in working practices, available? Would these have an impact upon managing the activity increases or in managing the service developments?

All of these possible solutions will be considered by finance staff in conjunction with service managers.

Patient Choice, the National Tariff and Payment by Results

Two major changes to the NHS, introduced in 2002, and due to be fully up and running by 2008, are Patient Choice and the Payment by Results. These are integrated systems for the commissioning and finance regimes and will have a fundamental impact on the administration of finances throughout the NHS.

Patient Choice

Patients are to be empowered and given an increased influence in their care decisions. This is to the extent that, at the point they are referred for treatment, usually by a GP, they will have a say in where they are referred.

The National Tariff and Payment by Results

The administration of finances will change as a result of patient choice and 'The Payment by Results' is the title given to this agenda. Whilst all the mechanisms and planning of PCTs, as discussed in this and the previous chapter, will remain, they will have to be made more fluid.

For instance, if a PCT's local acute Trust is struggling to match either the waiting times or quality of care of its neighbours, patients may choose to travel elsewhere for care. Whilst the PCT will have planned for the local Trust to receive the relevant funds, these will now have to be paid to the Trust the patient has chosen to travel to.

Assuming the overall plan for the PCT includes the expectation of this unit of activity, the plan will not have to be changed as the relevant sum of money will have been accounted for. The National Tariff assures the sum charged by the new Trust will be similar as it is a mechanism by which all providers will have to charge a set sum, albeit weighted for local issues.

This is a change to the previous system where PCT plans tended to include relatively rigid splits of activity and funds, based upon providers. The following worked example distinguishes between the old and new systems.

Worked Example

The total number of hip replacements within City PCT's plan is 100 for the year: 80 are to be provided at the local acute Trust, 15 at the neighbouring acute Trust and 5 in the wider area.

Under the old system, these splits would have led to the relevant sum of money being agreed to between commissioner and provider, and monthly payments would have been spread equally over the year. Only if the actual split or level of activity varied materially from this plan would changes to the payments have occurred.

Under Payment by Results, City PCT's opening plan will include the same splits between providers but also a mechanism whereby the splits can be altered, should the need arise. The 100 units of activity will remain the plan but, were the local acute Trust to suffer capacity pressures, City PCT and its providers' systems will be flexible enough for a transfer of some of the 80 hip replacements elsewhere. With this transfer of activity will follow a transfer of finances.

This is the key to the Payment by Results agenda. Rather than rigid monthly payments being made to providers based upon a total agreed at the beginning of the year through the Service Level Agreement, PCTs will need to constantly monitor the pattern of referrals and monthly payments will need to reflect this.

Partnership Arrangements

Joint Funds and Pooled Budgets

As discussed in Chapter 9, PCTs enter into Joint Fund and Pooled Budget arrangements with local authorities.

The purpose of these is to ensure a 'whole systems approach' in which commissioning and provider bodies with similar aims are able to make care decisions effectively. Some of the financial benefits are to reduce the bureaucratic costs as there will be one joint process and monitoring system rather than individual processes. There is also an increase in bargaining power by pooling the resources and SLAs.

Lead Commissioner and Host Purchaser Responsibilities

As with Joint Funds, this is a process in which bureaucratic and administrative efficiencies are achieved by PCTs working together as commissioners. Collective bargaining in SLA negotiations allows for more influence and ensures the best 'deal' for the PCT and its resident population.

A *host purchaser* is the PCT with the largest commissioning relationship within an NHS Trust. This PCT has sole responsibility for commissioning accident and emergency activity from the Trust, and the main responsibility for monitoring the provider and ensuring that its targets are met.

A *lead commissioner* is the PCT, within a collective of local PCTs, responsible for purchasing services on behalf of the collective and ensuring the best service and cost is achieved for the extended population. In most cases this tends to be an agreement between two or three neighbouring PCTs. However, for specialist services the number of PCTs included may increase. This is for services such as neonatal intensive care or medium secure mental health services where the level of activity per PCT is low but the unit costs are high (known as 'high cost, low volume' services). In such cases one PCT may host the service, employing the commissioning staff and providing the financial support, but those involved in providing the service work on behalf of all the member PCTs.

Who PCTs Commission From
A summary of the types of organisations PCTs commission from are:

- Acute NHS Trusts
- Mental health NHS Trusts
- Ambulance Trusts
- Other PCTs
- Local authorities
- Charitable and voluntary organisations
- Private sector

The Primary Care Trust as Provider

Community Health Services, Learning Difficulties, Continuing and Elderly Care

PCTs provide the bulk of these services to their resident populations. For community health services, which include District Nursing and Health Visiting, some services may be provided by neighbouring PCTs to residents living just outside their area. This caseload will be dealt with by commissioning.

The responsibility for the provision of learning difficulties and continuing and elderly care rests within individual PCTs. However, in the interests of efficiency, and of ensuring a holistic service, in practice one PCT may provide a full service to its own and its neighbour's populations.

General Practitioners, Dentists, Opticians/Opthalmicologists and Pharmacists

PCTs are charged with administering the provision of general medicine, dental, ophthalmic and pharmaceutical services to residents.

In practice, the practitioners of these services do not work for the PCT but the PCT provides much of the funds for their services and has to manage its budgets for this.

The GP Contract

A new contracting and therefore financial relationship between the NHS (in the form of PCTs) and GPs began on April 1st 2003 and will be functioning completely from April 1st 2004.

The Previous System

GPs are not employed by the NHS. Their relationship with the NHS is similar to that of an independent business. GP practices are private businesses, owned by the partners. The NHS, partly via the PCTs and partly via the Department of Health, pays them to provide services for NHS patients. Previously GPs practising under the general medical services (GMS) system received the majority of their income through a mechanism called Items of Service. This worked through the recording of data such as an individual GP's list size, the deprivation of the GP's catchment area and activity (or 'service items') carried out by the practice. The practice would then receive payments based upon this information, per item of service.

The New System

The new relationship is practice-based (as with the PMS contracts discussed in Chapter Nine) rather than individual GP-based and practices will receive income through four channels. These are the Global sum, Seniority payments, Enhanced Services payments and the Quality Framework payments.

Global Sum

The global sum is an amount per patient that is guaranteed to all practices and covers the essential services all GPs are expected to provide for their patients. The global sum will also include some additional services which practices (but not individual GPs) will be able to opt out of. The opt-outs, such as not providing an out of hours service directly, carry financial reductions on the basis of percentages of a practice's total global sum.

Within the global sum exists the Minimum Practice Income Guarantee. This only relates to funding areas within the global sum and is intended to ensure that GPs will not lose income as a result of moving from the old to the new system.

Global sums are reviewed by the Department of Health on a quarterly basis and payments are made through PCTs, based upon the latest validated information, for example 2004/05 Quarter 1 payments are based upon 2003/04 Quarter 4 data.

Seniority

These are increased payments made to practices depending upon the number of years their GPs have spent in the profession.

Enhanced Services Payments

These payments will be available to practices through commissioning agreements. Examples of enhanced services include programmes to improve access to GPs, influenza immunisations, preschool boosters and childhood immunisations. PCTs will commission these services from GPs, agreeing criteria for delivery of the services and a negotiated payment.

Quality Framework
Practices will obtain financial rewards for providing a quality service across a series of different areas within their health care. The system for this is that a practice will indicate which and what level of services they intend to provide. Points will be assigned to a practice for each quality achievement within these services, set against national criteria, and a further sum of money per point is paid to the practice. Failure to then achieve these quality standards will require a refund of that element of the quality framework payment.

The GP Contract and Financial Systems

The new GP contract brings with it the new payment systems described above, and with it the need for new monitoring systems within PCT finance in order to ensure that funding streams flow smoothly and GP practices receive the correct sums for the work they are commissioned to perform.

Monitoring Variances in PMS/GMS: How it is Done

There is no official system by which PCTs must monitor variances between the two contracting systems for general practice. However, as with all NHS Service Level Agreements, monitoring is essential to ensure that services are provided as agreed, and that variances are proactively managed and finances adjusted.

As mentioned above, the global sum monitoring mechanism is managed by the Department of Health with PCTs being informed of changes and the financial adjustments these require. However, for the other areas within the GP contract, and the sections of PMS contracts for which financial adjustments have been agreed in the event of activity or list size changes, the commissioning PCT will need its own mechanisms.

An example of how these might work is where changes in seniority, occur (when a GP passes from one range to the next due to an increasing number of years in service). The system may be for a practice to inform the PCT that a change is due in year. The PCT will then be able to adjust the financial baseline accordingly.

A further example is services with payments based on activity levels, such as enhanced services for the GP Contract. The PCT's monitoring team may access the actual level of activity of a practice at Month 6, compare this with the forecast likely level of activity for the same period, and then forecast the likely year-end total activity. The practice and the PCT will then be aware of whether this is in line with the agreed level in the contract and, if not, decide whether to adjust activity levels to bring the total in line by the end of the year or adjust the agreed financial baseline accordingly.

The method by which general practice activity is monitored is for the practice to 'log' the activity it performs electronically. This information is then sent to the PCT and a sample is validated, usually remotely but also via practice visits to check records.

Provider Services and the Finance Function

The commissioner/provider relationship is reversed for PCTs with the above services. The PCT is in this instance the provider of services, both to itself and, in some cases, to neighbours. As a result, the PCT produces budgets which total the element of their Resource Limit, identified for provision plus income from other organisations. This is then managed and monitored during the financial year to ensure compliance with the financial duty, mentioned in Chapter 9, to 'achieve full cost recovery for their provider functions'.

The Dual Role of Primary Care Trusts

As can be seen, a PCT has a complicated make-up. This includes the commissioning function for its resident population, and the provider function for community care, which incorporates the administration of all primary care.

Within these functions, a PCT may transfer some of its commissioning work to neighbouring PCTs, in Lead Commissioning agreements, and to local authorities via Joint Funds. Also, a provider function, such as learning difficulties, may be shared with neighbours.

Whilst the functions may be transferred, the responsibility for them is not. This means robust, detailed and accurate monitoring systems must be in place. The various models within the commissioning cycle and the provider-side budgeting system are the mechanisms by which this is achieved.

The financial successes of these dual PCT roles are overseen by the finance function but rely heavily on the prudence and management of the numerous managers and budget holders throughout the organisation. In this way, the funding which is available to PCTs can be used for the best benefit of the local population.

SELF-STUDY QUESTIONS

1. What are the benefits of Joint Funding arrangements with local authorities?

2. What is a host purchaser? Explain the circumstances in which a host purchaser may be used.

3. Who do PCTs commission from?

4. Indicate which of the following are 'provided by' and 'administered by' PCTs:

   Learning difficulties
   Dental services
   Pharmaceutical services
   District Nursing

Further Reading

Department of Health (October 2002) *Reforming NHS Financial Flows: Introducing Payment by Results*, DoH, London.

Department of Health (October 2003) *Building on the Best: Choice, Responsiveness and Equity in the NHS*, Cm 6079, DoH, London.

Department of Health (October 2004) *The NHS Improvement Plan: Putting People at the Heart of Public Services*, Cm 6268, DoH, London.

11

Foundation Hospitals

The Beginning of the End, or the End of the Beginning?

In the late Frank Sinatra's song 'And now the end is near, we face the final curtain …', from where he was standing, he saw the final curtain coming down.

To some people, and to some groups within the government, the proposal to introduce and to run foundation hospitals in England poses the potential threat of the curtain coming down on the National Health Service. For a variety of reasons, there has been fierce political opposition to the proposals, and in spite of defeats at the Labour Party Conference in October 2003, party managers pressed ahead and achieved the passage of appropriate legislation to implement foundation hospitals. On Wednesday, 19 November 2003 a House of Commons vote recorded 302 votes in favour, and 285 votes against, a majority for the government of 17 votes, at a time when their clear Commons' majority was 160, so the result was a tight squeeze, and was only achieved by the backing of Scottish and Welsh MPs, whose countries are not involved in the proposals.

The origin of foundation hospitals came from a visit by the then Secretary of State, Alan Milburn, to the Alcorcan hospital in Madrid in autumn 2001. The hospital was state-owned but run by private management. The advantages of independence allowed surpluses earned by a particular site to be recycled and reinvested for the benefit of that place. The idea of independently run hospitals within the NHS represented a middle ground between the previously considered options of a health service run wholly by the state or wholly by private companies.

Foundation Hospitals – The Essential Features

A foundation hospital essentially has to develop a cluster of skills around itself. These include:

- high standards of patient care
- involvement with and a connection to the local community, in which local community interests are directly represented in the governance arrangements
- high levels of skills in management
- sound financial management
- priority given to the health and safety of staff and patients.

If these conditions exist and are verifiable, then an existing Trust hospital can apply for foundation status. The first wave of potential foundation trusts amounted to 32 hospitals.

If foundation status is awarded, the hospital becomes self-governing and is not subject to the micro control exercised by the National Health Service. Whilst remaining part of the National Health Service, it will be able to retain revenue surpluses, and build up its internal strength without being weakened by the handing over of surpluses to a central source, (the Treasury), as happens at the moment with all other hospitals. Foundation status would also be achievable by PCTs, charities or private companies, so hospices or other specialised units could apply for this status.

What are the Main Political Objections to Foundation Status?

It is very significant that the idea of foundation hospitals came from Spain. It illustrates that the provision of health care is an international industry, and that the best minds in the world are facing the dilemma of how to provide care against a background of increasing demand and limited financial resources. The UK model of hospital provision started many years ago as one of local authority provision, and private provision. In the aftermath of the Second World War, when many UK cities and centres of population had to face the task of rebuilding essential services, the decision was taken to set up the National Health Service in which all buildings would be state-owned, and all planning would come under the single control of the Department of Health. This ensured that the service concentrated its efforts on standards of care and quality of service, linked to the building of facilities in a planned way so that waste and duplication of services were avoided.

With centralisation came other benefits such as rationalisation of pay and conditions for staff, and recognised routes to qualifications of doctors and nurses. The things which were required to make the system work were all in place, and that included research, buildings, and inspection, quality control, and community councils.

Successive decades from 1948 onwards had their characteristics: the 1950s saw improvements in health care, particularly among children and young people; the 1960s saw a big expansion in training of medical personnel; the 1970s were characterised by large building programmes of new hospitals; the 1980s by the building of more independently owned hospitals from the private sector, following a policy of liberalisation by the Conservative government, and the 1990s by a move towards faster treatment of patients, and reduction of waiting lists. In the view of the opponents to foundation hospitals, the record of the past showed that achievements were won slowly, but they were managed in such a way that the benefits were widespread. The perceived threat to the health service is that foundation hospitals may take the major share of resources and skills, with other hospitals being left behind. Potentially, this could be the start of a two-tier health system, where foundation status could have the effect of giving more resources to one tier, at the expense of, or detriment to the other, less fortunate tier. Staff may be attracted to the better pay and conditions of the foundation Trusts, which could lead to staff shortages or loss of morale in non-foundation sites. Also, foundation Trusts could potentially become a little too self-sufficient, and be unwilling to co-operate in joint working arrangements with other Trusts, to the detriment of the local community, in terms of reduced services being offered. All these disadvantages were perceived in the minds of people who had experience of previous reorganisations and feared the same thing happening again.

The Safeguards for Fairness, Appropriate Standards of Care and Measurement of Results

Compromises can be agreed on all these objections and the new arrangements will obviously have to be tuned and managed in such a way that there is fairness and equity between community users of the services and the management of the Trusts.

- The proposals for setting up the new foundation Trusts will ensure community representation in the board of governors.
- The Commission for Healthcare Audit and Inspection will have important supervisory access to all hospitals to ensure fairness, and demonstrable standards of care.
- The contracts set up between the hospitals and the local PCT will guarantee that foundation hospitals will receive the right amount of resources in line with previously agreed contract rates of financing for the workload they engage in.

The Context of the Changes

It may seem like a philosophical question, but how do you feel about the introduction of foundation hospitals? Why is such a change happening? What are the possible benefits?

The NHS was formed against the background of reconstruction of a country after the Second World War. Money and all other resources were in short supply. Central planning and control from the centre were seen as the most effective way forward. Central direction implied central funding: in the 1980's both political parties realised that the investment in certain major industries could not be made without putting up taxes to a very high level, and if that were so, then Britain's place as a manufacturing base would be threatened as other countries achieved lower costs of production. So, in pursuit of a low tax economy, governments' attention turned to pushing back the frontiers of the state, to reducing central influence and control in certain key industries; and one by one, large organisations which were dependent partly on government borrowing were transferred into the private sector. This was the process of 'privatisation' which took about 30 years. As a consequence, central government was no longer responsible for raising these organisations' capital or long-term loans for investment and development. Their requirements dropped out of the Public Sector Borrowing Requirement and consequently, direct taxes, measured by rates of income tax on earned income, were able to fall.

While this process was on-going, the health service was regarded as a special case – a monopoly provider of an essential service – and possible scenarios were considered for change. Each time they ran up against considerable opposition to change. Some of the changes proposed simply lacked the political majority to carry them through, and sometimes the politicians lacked detailed knowledge of the way the service worked. To change the whole system by radical changes was simply not feasible, without large scale political embarrassment, or administrative collapse.

Two important things happened: recognising that the health service was a very important special case, the New Labour government, who took over after the defeat of the Conservatives in 1997, preserved the spending plans of the previous government and for roughly three years maintained the spending power in real terms, without adding to the total amount available. The effect of this was that waiting lists and waiting times increased, and doctors realised that if no more money was coming forward for hospital care, a better strategy would be to divert money into primary care. By earlier diagnosis and more resources at a local level, there could be perceived improvements in the health of the nation where more people could develop a healthier lifestyle, with support from local GP practices, rather than receive hospital care at a later stage, which was bound to be more expensive. The Primary Care Groups, which linked like-minded GPs in the early 1990s, were formally set up as Primary Care Trusts, and a policy announcement made that in future up to 70% of all health service resources would pass through the PCTs.

So, the freezing of money for three years, in terms of public expenditure, had the effect of producing a completely new health care delivery system, based on PCTs.

The second thing which happened was linked to the pressure on major hospitals, and that was the liberalisation of rules in the 1970s about who provides hospital beds. The Conservative government had allowed some expansion in the building of private hospitals, and private sector firms had specialised in building local facilities for elective surgery where insurance firms and private funds would settle their patients' bills. In the three years of no increase in public funds, it was clear that the growth in private beds could not absorb all the demand: the partial solution of more private beds was not the answer to the increasing demand on the health service. At the end of the three-year period of freeze, the Cabinet agreed to year on year increases which were three times the rate of inflation: so substantial new money came in, and continued to come into the health budget. Micro control, of inspection and financial verification, was directed so that definite benefits would be seen to be gained from this new money. Benefits such as a redesigned and faster degree programme for doctors; a new GP contract; new substantial hospital building programmes; new community treatment centres; new local hospitals; more investment in imaging systems and electronic scanners; more investment in information technology, medical records and support systems.

The increased investment in hospitals and PCT assets will take some years to come to fruition, but it is clear that the National Health Service is the chosen vehicle for delivery of health care. The monitoring of what is achieved will be the subject of intense Parliamentary scrutiny, and measures of performance exist to underline where Trusts have performed up to expectations, or in some cases, where extra managerial effort is required. Sanctions can be applied in the form of withdrawal of funding if a Trust fails on specific aspects of its work.

Where to Now?

As the time of writing this edition, the Scottish Parliament and the Welsh Assembly have shown no interest in pursuing the idea of foundation hospitals. Since devolution, these assemblies have power to direct the education and health of their constituents. Scottish cities have a greater proportion of hospital beds per head of population than the average for the rest of the UK. They have a smaller proportion of private beds and a larger concentration of teaching hospitals, so the intention in Scotland has been to follow the model of the NHS as the predominant provider of care: there appears to be no enthusiasm to throw out what already exists in favour of foundation hospitals. Similar conditions exist in Wales, but cross-border arrangements with English hospitals which have a tradition of treating patients from North and Central Wales are additionally used – subject to an appropriate financial adjustment for the costs involved. The Welsh Assembly has no plans to move any of its hospitals towards foundation status.

The Advantages of Foundation Status and the Benefits From It

The Impact of Local Financial Autonomy

In a system which has been centrally controlled, there is an inevitable delay in processing and implementing large investment decisions. Foundation status, achieved by Trusts which have already achieved three stars in their annual review process, will be more financially independent of the Department of Health. In addition to having local accountable management, with new boards of governors and community representation to reflect local needs and aspirations, foundation Trusts will be able to borrow money, within agreed limits, from banks to promote local capital programmes. They will be able to retain the proceeds of sales of land, and to invest these proceeds in local schemes to enhance services. They will also be able to gain funds from central development budgets where a national scheme or initiative is being funded centrally.

This gives them more financial autonomy over expansion and investment in services. To this extent, financial autonomy is a reflection of local needs and priorities, and stops the process of assets being sold off, and the money used for non-health expenditure, from continuing to occur. From the government's point of view, the foundation status will result in more capital expenditure in the foundation hospitals originating in the private sector, and no longer counting as part of the Public Sector Borrowing Requirement. As a result, the size of debt which the government is responsible for will not necessarily increase proportionately to the increase in facilities, as the burden of debt is being carried by bankers rather than by the government. So, provided there are mechanisms in place to monitor outcomes and outputs from foundation hospitals, there seems to be no apparent disadvantage in giving them more local autonomy.

Managing Information Systems

Having gained more autonomy, or control over their direction and capital programmes, what other possible benefits are likely to arise? In any centrally controlled system, there is the problem of integrating all financial and operational information into a single understandable system. In the past, government ministers have only been able to answer specific questions in Parliament if their back-up ministries could provide the information. Gaps in the system existed, and the task of getting sufficient information to justify a change in policy was an essential part of the political process. In the future case of local foundation hospitals, they will benefit from being able to invest in systems which satisfy their own requirements, and it will be far easier and cheaper to obtain locally based support systems. From a staff point of view, if a local site owns the information, it becomes possible to respond quickly and to report factually to managers on the actual situation. Not only is the governance of foundation hospitals being devolved to a local level but, by implication, the ownership of information is being devolved to those most interested in using it – the local managers and staff.

Foundation hospitals will not require any changes in accounting, or in accounting principles, but they will require staff to be aware of how information is generated, how it is processed and reported; and the means of interpreting it and using it will be at a local level. To this extent, the creation of foundation hospitals is empowering local people to generate and use information which is directly relevant to their local situation. Rather than being collated for transmission outside the hospital, information will become useful to daily, weekly and monthly workloads.

Consequently, some part of the transition towards foundation hospitals will involve looking at current information systems, and finding out how they can be improved, or enhanced. Staff training will need to be developed which can equip people with the skills and knowledge required to make a good contribution to the recording of data, and ensuring that what is recorded locally is an accurate portrayal of activities, costs, and revenues. Local measurement systems will be easier to manage if their boundaries are well defined, and people operating within those boundaries are clear as to what is expected of them.

Foundation hospitals therefore represent a springboard for the future, and a new beginning for devolved, locally autonomous health services.

Further Reading

Hunter D (2003) Back to the Future, *Public Money and Management*, **23**(4): 211–13.

Mohan J (2003) *Reconciling Equity and Choice? Foundation Hospitals and the future of the NHS.* Catalyst Working Paper, Catalyst, London.

Useful Websites

www.SocietyGuardian.co.uk   Butler P and Gardner S, Q & A Foundation Trusts *Guardian*, 13 November 2002

www.SocietyGuardian.co.uk   Shifrin T, Q & A Foundation Hospitals *Guardian*, 19 November 2003

www.hospital.org.uk Guys and St. Thomas's Hospital NHS Trust Website: one of the first foundation Trusts in the UK

www.news.independent.co.uk Laurence J, Public to be offered £1 shares in new foundation hospitals *Independent* 14 March 2003

www.news.bbc.co.uk Contributors from the Public at large *Are foundation hospitals a good solution?* 25 November 2003

12

Moving Towards Devolved Hospitals and Payment by Results

In the document *Delivering the NHS Plan* (DoH, April 2002), there is this statement:

> It is time to move beyond the 1940s monolithic top down centralised NHS towards a devolved health service, offering wider choice and greater diversity bound together by common standards, tough inspection and NHS values.

What does a 'devolved health service' mean, and how would it be achieved? Certain steps have been taken towards giving large hospitals a direct link into the communities they serve, by representation, by appointment and by the governance arrangements. The idea of Primary Care Groups, which were formed by doctors acting together in a local arrangement, became so attractive to central government that within a relatively short time legislation was successfully introduced in Parliament to form Primary Care Trusts. These Trusts are a pivotal point in delivering patient care and, as they relate to a geographical area which is clearly identified, are a genuine attempt to give local communities a role in what was previously a 'top down' administratively imposed system. So, PCTs are a starting point in a devolved local health system.

Foundation Trusts go one step further. By their record of satisfactory achievement, independently verified, they can claim a status of being independent, or autonomous, in their day-to-day management. They have more financial freedom, in the form of the retention of revenue surpluses, access to commercial lending through banks for capital projects, and local governance which is linked to community representation and community investment.

The Chancellor's Budget of 2002 announced a five-year sustained programme of revenue funding which averaged 7.4% per annum increase in real terms for the NHS. The PCTs, as the commissioners of health care, can enter into contracts to obtain the volume of care they require through annual 'block' agreements with hospital Trusts.

In a Consultation Paper *Reforming NHS Financial Flows: Payments by Results* (October 2002), the idea of changing the basis of contracts was put forward. The proposed change reflects what is happening in other European countries, and elsewhere, where there is a mixed economy of public and private health care. Notably France, Germany, the Netherlands, Italy, the Scandinavian countries, Canada, the United States and Australia have similar arrangements. Instead of having an annual block contract between the PCT and the provider of care, the new system would have an agreed national tariff of prices for work done within the UK, and the prices in the national tariff would be derived from statistical data submitted by hospitals on their actual costs of surgical procedures. For the system of a national tariff of prices to work, the government would publish in advance the prices for 15 HRGs, or 'health care resource groups'. These prices would be modified by the effect of local expenditure factors, for example, to reflect high costs of living in some areas. The local adjustment would be called the 'market forces factor'. The target date for this national tariff to be introduced is April 2005.

In 2004/05 the 15 original HRGs would have an additional 33 specialties or procedures added to the list of prices, making a total of 48 HRGs, and from 2005/06 nearly all specialties would be on a cost- and volume-based contract using local tariff prices. Over a three-year period of transition, the local adjustment or 'market forces factor' would be phased out, and by 2008/09, there would be a set of tariffs which would apply irrespective of where a procedure was carried out. Between 2005/06 and 2008/09, hospitals would have to be conscious of how their costs compared to the nationally set tariff, and if they were high cost hospitals, there would be internal pressure to get costs down to within an acceptable range of the national tariff. There would also be flexibility within the system as commissioners (the PCTs) could enter into contracts to use more than a single provider, and those providers with lower costs would naturally be more ready to enter into contracts. The national tariff would encourage efficiency within providers.

Hospital Trusts granted foundation status would start from April 2004, and any additional work over their original workload would be reimbursed at tariff prices. They would therefore be one year ahead of the rest of the NHS system in implementing tariff prices.

Primary Care Trusts would use tariff pricing from April 2005, and their purchasing power, using tariffs, would be guaranteed to be equivalent to their purchasing power under the previous arrangements of block contracts.

What Are the Benefits of a Tariff System?

From the viewpoint of central government, the government would have control of the volume of authorised work, by agreeing with PCTs the needs of their areas, through the annual assessment of population trends and diagnosis patterns (the resource allocation process). The government would also direct or control the unit price of all the procedures included in the HRGs.

The PCTs would have a level of certainty over their funding for a full year in advance and possibly longer, and would have sufficient flexibility to purchase the volume of care they required from foundation hospitals, local non foundation Trusts, or from the private sector.

Within the system, patients would be able to choose where and by whom they were to be treated, as all the providers would be capable of providing care for a fixed price rechargeable to the PCT. In many ways, some commentators have remarked, it is a return to the internal market which operated briefly in the 1990s, but with this difference: this time the volume is predetermined, and the price is an average price across the country, to which all providers have to work.

The Units of Measurement of Patient Care for a Tariff-based System

A set of technical papers (September 2003 and June 2004), see website at end of chapter, have stated how an in-patient stay in hospital should be counted. Deciding upon an appropriate measure is important because the collection of data within a hospital, which provides the basis for funding, must be on a rational and firm set of rules.

The funding in 2003/04 is based on the number of finished consultant episodes, known as FCEs. So, an FCE covers the period of each in-patient stay where the responsibility for care is held by an individual consultant. There is a new FCE where a patient passes to a different consultant, so there can be more than one FCE. There is another term, an FFCE, which means the first finished consultant episode, where the sequence of dealing with the patient is reflected in the measure used.

In most countries where a system of tariff pricing is used, the measure adopted for counting patient care is a 'provider spell' (this occurs where the care a patient receives by a single Trust between admission and discharge (or death) is known as a 'spell').

At present, hospitals use FCE as the building blocks for collecting and storing data on in-patients. The technical papers in July 2003 indicated that there will have to be a gradual transition towards using 'provider spells' as the basis for counting and for funding. The target date for achieving the definition and use of 'provider spells' is 2004/05, one year before to the full implementation year of 2005/06.

The Challenge

From a clinical point of view, the speed of improvement in clinical diagnosis, treatment and discharge is increasing. The improvement in electronics, in imaging, in drug and treatment regimes, and in surgery is something which is worldwide. The administrative system, wherever it is based, has to deal with different administrative arrangements and changes in management style and requirements. Sometimes these changes are internally driven, sometimes externally imposed. Reporting systems have to deal with the past, the present and the future. The counting systems may be under different rules for different years, making comparisons between years fairly difficult to achieve. Does the past matter if we are moving into the future? It will matter if there are gaps in our knowledge of the past. Accounting systems have to handle last year, this year, and next year all at the same time, in money values that are changing.

It is clear that 'Payment by Results' or the introduction of tariff-based pricing is a really big administrative challenge in the timescale allowed. The benefits of devolved management and resource control at a local level will liberate central government of much detailed control, but in doing so will transfer a vast amount of work to foundation Trusts, non-foundation Trusts, and to Primary Care Trusts.

The big question will be: Are there sufficient numbers of skilled staff to handle the transition from a system which provided figures for use outside the hospital, by government, to a system which generates and uses the information it produces to inform local decision-makers, and ensure the financial survival of a local hospital, whether it is non-foundation, or foundation? All this is happening at a time of structural change in the status of hospitals, when senior management time is engaged on preparing for the consequences of applying for foundation status.

The need for information before the arrangements for tariff pricing become 'live' will require a vast amount of work, and most of this will be within hospitals and in PCTs. The purpose of this book has been to give an appreciation of scale and purpose of the changes. The Nuffield Trust commissioned a report by international health specialists in 2002, and their conclusion was that the changes were 'the most ambitious, comprehensive, and intentionally-funded national initiative to improve health-care quality in the world'. The fact that funding is part of the change indicates that there is a recognition that changes cannot take place without the earmarking of resources

The intention of this book is to guide the reader through the changes and to indicate where financial considerations are part of the process of change. In the past, the job of learning about finance in the health service has been like peeling an onion: many layers of understanding, frustration, and a painful process to the observer. The authors hope that this book will have lessened the pain, and that readers will feel more confident about the changes, and comfortable with the financial strategies and techniques being used.

SELF-STUDY QUESTIONS

1. How will hospitals achieve efficiency savings during the period of transition from local prices to the prices set in the national tariff for HRGs? Identify some of the ways in which hospitals can achieve efficiency savings.

2. Distinguish between an FCE, an FFCE, and a 'spell' as a means of counting inpatients. What is the significance of these terms against the background of the national tariff for HRGs?

Further Reading

Department of Health (2002) *Delivering the NHS Plan,* Cm 5503, DoH, London.
Nuffield Trust (2002) Series No. 6, *Future Challenges for the NHS: An International Perspective on the 50th Anniversary,* Nuffield Trust, London.
Plumridge, N (2003) Payment by Numbers, *Public Finance,* September 19–25 2003, **20–3**.

Useful Website

www.dh.gov.uk/nhsfinancialreforms/technicalpapers:

Technical Guidance for 2004/2005 (13 April 2004) Guidance about operating the new financial system, plus methodological and technical information about how the National Tariff was reached.
Payment by Results (30 January 2004) Changes following the publication of the consulation papers *Reforming NHS Financial Flows.*
2003–2004 Spell Uplift (24 June 2004) Details of the methodology for a spell-based tariff.

Appendix 1

Table of Discounting Factors

Present value of £1 received after _n_ years discounted at _i_%

_i_ _n_	1	2	3	4	5	6	7	8	9	10
1	.9901	.9804	.9709	.9615	.9524	.9434	.9346	.9259	.9174	.9091
2	.9803	.9612	.9426	.9246	.9070	.8900	.8734	.8573	.8417	.8264
3	.9706	.9423	.9151	.8890	.8638	.8396	.8163	.7938	.7722	.7513
4	.9610	.9238	.8885	.8548	.8227	.7921	.7629	.7350	.7084	.6830
5	.9515	.9057	.8626	.8219	.7835	.7473	.7130	.6806	.6499	.6209
6	.9420	.8880	.8375	.7903	.7402	.7050	.6663	.6302	.5963	.5645

_i_ _n_	11	12	13	14	15	16	17	18	19	20
1	.9009	.8929	.8850	.8772	.8696	.8621	.8547	.8475	.8403	.8333
2	.8116	.7929	.7831	.7695	.7561	.7432	.7305	.7182	.7062	.6944
3	.7312	.7118	.6931	.6750	.6575	.6407	.6244	.6068	.5934	.5787
4	.6587	.6355	.6133	.5921	.5718	.5523	.5337	.5158	.4987	.4823
5	.5935	.5674	.5428	.5194	.4972	.4731	.4561	.4371	.4190	.4019
6	.5346	.5066	.4803	.4556	.4323	.4104	.3910	.3704	.3521	.3349

Appendix 2

Exercises and Activities

Practical Exercise: Preparing a Small Budget

Exercise One

Assume that you are responsible for providing a diabetic advisory service in a PCT. From the following details, prepare a budget for a full year, based on the information available.

West Coast Primary Care Trust (WCPCT) employs two diabetic nurses, and each of them for three days per week carries out one-hour appointments with patients who have been identified as having Diabetes Type 2. The first appointment is to explain the nature of the condition to the patient, and to look at issues surrounding diet. The follow-up interview is to deal with questions arising from the first appointment, and to look at lifestyle issues. On the remaining two days of the week, the nurses are involved in visiting practices, and training junior nurses; their costs for these days are charged to the training budget of WCPCT.

The two diabetic nurses spend their three days between three GP practices: Gateway practice is run by Dr Singh, Riverside practice is run by Dr Talk, Parkland practice is run by Dr Warble. It is estimated that on each working day there will be six appointments arranged for each nurse, and in a normal working week they will spend a whole day at each of the three practices.

The diabetic nurse scale is currently £14,692–£16,520 per annum. Employers' National Insurance contributions amount to 11% of gross pay.

Required:

(a) Calculate the total annual budget of the diabetic nurse service, using the above data, and indicate how much is rechargeable to the three practices, and how much is rechargeable to the WCPCT training budget.
(b) Calculate the annual amount chargeable to Gateway practice, Riverside practice, and Parkland practice.
(c) At the end of the first year, the actual volume of appointments carried out was as follows:

Gateway   35% of the total number of appointments
Riverside   35% of the total number of appointments
Parkland   30% of the total number of appointments

In addition, the PCT had paid out a total of £480 in travelling expenses for the two nurses, and had paid for a total of £670 for professional training courses which were not estimated in the original budget in (a).

Calculate how the final costs for the year should be shared out between the GP practices of Gateway, Riverside, and Parkland. Assuming that the practices had paid their share of costs on the basis of the original budget, how much of a financial adjustment should there be to close the accounts for the year on the basis of the actual costs?

(d) Identify some of the points which may possibly need to be resolved in the preparation of a budget such as this.

Practical Exercise: Preparing a Budget With Recharges to Other Users

Exercise Two

The Imaging and X-ray department of a hospital in Bristol has an annual workload of approximately 8,000 cases per year.

The costs of consumable items, mainly X-ray film, files, pockets and plates are:

£22 for a full plate
£12 for a half plate
£7 for a quarter plate

The annual number of cases is estimated as:

1,500 full plate exposures
3,000 half plate exposures
3,500 quarter plate exposures

Four radiographers are employed full-time in the Imaging and X-ray service, and their pay scales are within the range £17,665–£21,325 per annum. Employers' National Insurance contributions amount to 11% of gross pay.

Required:

(a) Calculate the total budget for a full year of the Imaging and X-ray consumables and staff costs.
(b) At the end of the year, it was found that, as in previous years, a small proportion of cases had been referred to the hospital from a hospital in Gloucester, and also one in South Wales.
The respective caseloads were:

	Gloucester	South Wales
Full plate	200	100
Half plate	150	50
Quarter plate	300	100

Calculate the recharges which should be made to Gloucester and to South Wales on the basis of the above number of cases.
(c) How much of the service costs should remain in Bristol, after the end of year recharges to other users?
(d) Consider the role of the budget holder in managing a budget such as this, and briefly identify some of the issues which the budget holder would have to resolve.

Comparing Actual Expenditure and Income at a Point Six Months Through the Year with the Full-year Budget

Exercise Three

From the following data, calculate the financial position of Docklands NHS Trust for the six-month period from 1 April to 30 September.

Annual budget (twelve-month estimate)	£000
Category A income	80,000
Category B income	8,000
Category C income	12,000
Pay	60,000
Non-pay	30,000
Capital charges	10,000

Actual figures up to 30 September (a point six months through the financial year):

Category A income	40,000
Category B income	4,500
Category C income	5,800
Pay	29,800
Non-pay	15,400
Capital charges	5,000

Method:
This analysis can be done either by using a calculator, or by a spreadsheet.
Set out four columns to show:

- The annual full-year budget figure for each item
- The portion of the annual budget which should have been spent in the first six months
- The actual figures of income and expenditure for the first six months
- The difference (known as the variance) between the budgeted six-month figure (the amount expected to be received or spent in the first six months) and the actual figure (the amount definitely recorded as having been received, or spent, in the first six months).

Required:

(a) Prepare an analysis of the figures.
(b) Comment upon the figures.

Specialty Costing – Working Out the Total Costs of Hospital Departments

Exercise Four

From the following data, calculate the direct, indirect and overhead costs of the following hospital for the current full financial year.

Brightsea NHS Trust provides three specialties on a single site – ENT, Orthopaedics and General medical. It employs two consultants in ENT, two in Orthopaedics and one in General medical.

The Physiotherapy department employs three staff who work in two teams. One member covers ENT whilst the other two cover Orthopaedics.

The cost of the Human Resources department is £100,000 per annum, and the cost of the Finance department is £200,000 per annum. Analysis on the respective workloads of the Human Resources and Finance Departments indicates that the recharges should be as follows:

Human Resources
- to ENT £33,400
- to Orthopaedic £43,800
- to General medical £22,800

Finance
- to ENT £64,600
- to Orthopaedic £88,200
- to General medical £47,200

The nursing complement on each ward within the hospital is as follows:

Grade G × 1
Grade E × 2
Grade C × 3

There are two ENT, three Orthopaedic and two General medical wards within the hospital.

The two theatres (one ENT and one Orthopaedic) each employ the following nursing staff:

Grade G × 1
Grade E × 3
Grade C × 1

Information from the Pathology systems shows that the monthly number of tests requested is:

ENT	200
Orthopaedics	100
General medical	400

The average cost of each test is £10

The total cost of heating and lighting is £40,000 per annum. The total floor area of the specialties is:

ENT	3,000 square metres
Orthopaedics	5,000 square metres
General medical	2,000 square metres

The information from the Pharmacy system shows the annual cost of drugs for each specialty is:

ENT	£40,000
Orthopaedics	£40,000
General medical	£100,000

X-ray tests are requested at a cost of £20 each. The monthly number of requests made by each specialty is:

ENT	200
Orthopaedics	600
General medical	200

The Orthopaedics department spends £100,000 per annum on prostheses.

The cost of the Dietetic department is £40,000 per annum. 80% of the resources are allocated to General medical with the remaining 20% allocated to ENT.

The capital charges (land, buildings and equipment) for each specialty per annum is :

ENT	£180,000
Orthopaedics	£200,000
General medical	£120,000

Staffing costs (based on gross pay, employers' National Insurance and associated salary expenses) per annum:

Consultants	£100,000
Grade G	£40,000
Grade E	£30,000
Grade C	£20,000
Physotherapist	£20,000

Required: Calculate the cost of the hospital from the data given.

Method: Prepare four columns, by using either a calculator or a spreadsheet, one column for each specialty, and one for the total.

List the direct costs first, those which are directly related to the specialty's function, and total them. Then list the indirect costs which can be shared between specialties on a reasonably fair basis, for example by their usage of a service. Total these to give total indirect costs per specialty.

Finally, put in the overhead costs shared on a suitable basis of allocation between the specialties. Use any relevant information given in the question.

Add together the direct, indirect and overhead costs for each specialty.

Working Out Contract Prices Based on Actual Costs

Exercise Five

Using the total costs worked out in Exercise Four, which arrived at the total costs of the ENT, Orthopaedic and General medical specialties in the Brightsea Hospital, use the following information to work out the contract price for patients referred from the two neighbouring PCTS, whose data are as follows:

	In-patient activity rates at Brightsea Hospital from Riverside PCT	In-patient activity rates at Brightsea Hospital from Docklands PCT
ENT	350	200
Orthopaedics	356	150
General medical	370	100

Required: Calculate, using a calculator, or a spreadsheet, the cost for each referral based on the total costs for the hospital, calculated in Exercise Four, which is derived by dividing the specialty cost by the total activity in that specialty.

Then, calculate the value of the contract chargeable to each PCT by multiplying the number of referrals by the unit cost of each specialty.

Volume Changes in a Contract

Exercise Six

What is the extra cost on the contract value of Riverside PCT if it purchases another additional 25 Orthopaedic episodes?

All the episodes will involve the insertion of a prosthesis into the patient's joint.

Method. Using the cost per referral (cost per in-patient) for orthopaedic patients from the calculations in Exercise Five, calculate the cost of 25 more in-patients at the same price, plus the additional variable costs of drugs and prostheses on the cost of the Orthopaedic caseload from Riverside. The prices for other specialties, ENT and General medical, remain unchanged.

Calculating a Salaries and Wages Budget for a New Department

Exercise Seven

Clydebank Hospital is due to open a new six-bed critical care unit on 1 October, 2004. It will be staffed by:

2 Nurse consultants, critical care Band 8A
8 Specialist nurses, critical care Band 7
5 Qualified nurses Band 5
2 Medical secretaries Band 3 and one half-time medical secretary (supervisor) Band 4

Required:

(a) Identify some of the issues which will need to be resolved before the budget for this new department is prepared, either in discussions with managers, or with the budget holders.

(b) Prepare a salaries and wages budget for the financial year
2004/05, and also a budget for 2005/06 for the critical care unit.
Show the basis for your calculations clearly.

The following information on pay bands is given to you.

The new pay bands from April 2003

Band	Minimum(£)	Maximum(£)	Examples of staff who fall into each band
1	10,425	11,457	Domestic assistant, invoice clerk, porter
2	11,148	13,832	Admissions clerk, ambulance call taker, cook
3	12,851	15,380	Consumer services officer, cook (supervisor), medical secretary
4	15,019	18,064	Medical secretary (supervisor), multi-skilled maintenance technician, works officer (engineering maintenance)
5	17,548	22,709	Ambulance paramedic, qualified nurse, dietitian
6	20,954	28,386	District nursing sister, midwife, specialist therapists and nurses
7	25,290	33,341	Ambulance service area manager, biochemist, specialist nurses and nurse managers
8A	32,257	38,709	Principal clinical scientist (medical physics), nurse consultant critical care
8B	37,573	46,451	Consultant midwife, nurse consultant critical care
8C	45,212	55,741	Consultant clinical scientist (biochemistry, medical physics), consultant midwife
8D	54,193	67,096	Consultant clinical scientist (biochemistry, medical physics)

Figures will rise by 3.225% in April 2004 and in April 2005. Band eight has four categories.
Some jobs in band eight can be placed in more than one category, depending on duties

Solutions to Exercises and Activities

Exercise One

(a) Salary and National Insurance
     (based on the mid-point of the scale)   £
     $2 \times (16,520 + 14,692)/2 = 2 \times £15,606$ = 31,212
     National Insurance contributions = $.11 \times 31,212$ =   3,433
                                                                          34,645

(b) Annual amount chargeable to practices:
     Gateway practice $1/5 \times £34,645$ 6,929
     Riverside practice $1/5 \times £34,645$ 6,929
     Parkland practice $1/5 \times £34,645$ 6,929

The proportion for each practice is one fifth of the hours available each week as 3 days are spent in practices, and the remaining 2 days are charged to the training activities budget of WCPCT.

(c)		**Total**	**3/5 for practices**	**2/5 for WCPCT**
		£	£	£
Original estimate as in (a)		34,645	20,787	13,858
Unforeseen expenditure				
Additional costs				
Travelling expenses	480			
Professional training				
courses	670			
		1,150	1,150	
		35,795	**21,937**	**13,858**

	Original estimate £	Actual expenditure £	Year-end adjustment £
Gateway	6,929	7,678 [.35 × 21,937]	749 to pay
Riverside	6,929	7,678 [.35 × 21,937]	749 to pay
Parkland	6,929	6,581 [.30 × 21,937]	348 refund
	20,787	**21,937**	**1,150**

(d)

(i) Salary Costs

On what basis should salary costs be put into the budget? Using the mid-point assumes that both nurses will be appointed and with a result that their pay will be at the mid-point of the scale, but this may not be the case. If they are both experienced, and long-serving staff, it is quite possible that their pay will be closer to the maximum on the scale.

If the budget was reworked on the maximum of the pay scale, and not on the mid-point, there would be additional salary costs of 2 × £914 = £1,828, plus additional national insurance contributions of £201, a total of £2,029 per year. This would increase the original budget for each practice by £406 (that is, the extra full year costs of £2,029 spread between Gateway, Riverside and Parkland, and £812 to the training budget).

(ii) Overhead Costs

This year there has been unforeseen expenditure on travelling expenses and professional training costs. As these were not envisaged at the time of the original budget, they have resulted in extra charges, shared between the three practices, of £1,150.

In preparing next year's budget, some thought needs to be given towards building into the budget a figure for essential extra costs, for example travelling expenses, and possibly more training expenditure, if both these items are to be charged to the service next year. If this is done at the stage of preparing estimates, there will be no need for extra payments at year-end.

Exercise Two

(a) Total budget

Consumable costs: £

Full plate	1,500 × £22	33,000
Half plate	3,000 × £12	36,000
Quarter plate	3,500 × £7	24,500
		93,500

Staff costs: £

4 × (17,665 + 21,325)/2 = 4 x £19,495   77,980

National Insurance .11 × 77,980   8,578

                                                                86,558

Total budget for consumable costs and staff costs: **180,058**

(b)

Recharge to Gloucester:	£
200 × £22	4,400
150 × £12	1,800
300 × £7	2,100
	8,300

Recharge to South Wales	£
100 × £22	2,200
50 × £12	600
100 × £7	700
	3,500

(c) Costs remaining in Bristol will be: £180,058 – £8,300 – £3,500 = £168,258.

(d) This is a demand-led service: it is not easy to predict the number of cases per year.

- Need for accurate recording of workload.
- Need to establish whether the other users are going to pay for consumables only, as it seems fair to reimburse the hospital for work done. If either of the other users becomes more dominant in terms of demand, then perhaps some additional charges

should be made, but at the moment, their use of the service is relatively small.

● Need to establish whether the mid-point of the scale is a reasonable assumption. If it is not, then the budget will be overspent, and it needs to be designed at a realistic figure based on the four staff employed and their rates of pay.

Exercise Three

Calculation of the financial position of Docklands NHS Trust after six months of the year have elapsed.

£000s

	ANNUAL BUDGET			BUDGET TO 30 Sep	ACTUAL TO 30 Sep	VARIANCE TO 30 Sep
INCOME						
A	£	80,000	.5 x 80,000	£ 40,000	£ 40,000	
B	£	8,000	.5 x 8,000	£ 4,000	£ 4,500	£ 500
C	£	12,000	.5 x 12,000	£ 6,000	£ 5,800	-£ 200
TOTAL INCOME:	£	100,000		£ 50,000	£ 50,300	£ 300
EXPENDITURE						
PAY	£	60,000	.5 x 60,000	£ 30,000	29,800	£ 200
NON-PAY	£	30,000	.5 x 30,000	£ 15,000	15,400	-£ 400
CAPITAL CHARGES	£	10,000	.5 x 10,000	£ 5,000	5,000	£ -
TOTAL EXPENDITURE:	£	100,000		£ 50,000	50,200	-£ 200
TOTAL FOR THE TRUST AS A WHOLE	0			0	100	100

Comments on the figures:

1. A minus sign in the last column on the right indicates an 'adverse' variance: this means that figures are worse than expected. Thus, the income from category C of £5,800,000 is lower than the anticipated income, which was estimated at £6,000,000 which is an adverse variance of £200,000 … a shortfall of income.

2. Similarly, non-pay expenditure is showing an 'adverse' variance of £400,000 meaning that costs in non-pay items have been greater than expected, by an overspending of £400,000.

3. These two items would need to have the greatest attention paid to them in the remaining months of the financial year, in order to get the budget back on track.
4. Overall, the Trust is in a favourable position of being £100,000 in surplus at the end of six months to 30 September. This is because income has been £300,000 higher than expected, and expenditure is £200,000 higher than expected, leaving an overall surplus of £100,000.

Note: The various categories of income in this question are:
Category A: Patient-related income that does not vary according to patient activity
Category B: Patient-related income that does vary according to patient activity
Category C: Non-patient-related income

Exercise Four

Calculation of the cost for a full year of specialties in the Brightsea NHS Hospital Trust.

	ENT	ORTHOPAEDICS	GENERAL MEDICAL	TOTAL
DIRECT COSTS	£	£	£	£
CONSULTANTS	200,000	200,000	100,000	500,000
WARD NURSING	320,000	480,000	320,000	1,120,000
THEATRE NURSING	150,000	150,000	0	300,000
DRUGS	40,000	40,000	100,000	180,000
PROSTHESES	0	100,000	0	100,000
TOTAL	**710,000**	**970,000**	**520,000**	**2,200,000**
INDIRECT COSTS				
PHYSIOTHERAPY	20,000	40,000	0	60,000
PATHOLOGY	24,000	12,000	48,000	84,000
X RAY	48,000	144,000	48,000	240,000
DIETETICS	8,000	0	32,000	40,000
TOTAL	**100,000**	**196,000**	**128,000**	**424,000**
OVERHEAD COSTS				
HUMAN RESOURCES	33,400	43,800	22,800	100,000
FINANCE	64,600	88,200	47,200	200,000
HEATING & LIGHTING	12,000	20,000	8,000	40,000
CAPITAL CHARGES	180,000	200,000	120,000	500,000
TOTAL	**290,000**	**352,000**	**198,000**	**840,000**
TOTAL	**1,100,000**	**1,518,000**	**846,000**	**3,464,000**

Exercise Five

Calculation of the cost of each referral in each of the three specialties at Brightsea Hospital.

		ENT		ORTHOPAEDICS	GENERAL MEDICINE		TOTAL	
		£		£	£		£	
Specialty cost from Exercise Four analysis		1,100,000		1,518,000	846,000		3,464,000	
Number of referrals in-patient activity		550		506	470		1,526	
Cost per in-patient		**2,000**		**3,000**	**1,800**			

Value of contract with Riverside PCT: £

ENT	350 x £2,000	700,000
Orthopaedics	356 x £3,000	1,068,000
General medical	370 x £1,800	666,000
TOTAL:		**2,434,000**

Value of contract with Docklands PCT: £

ENT	200 x £2,000	400,000
Orthopaedics	150 x £3,000	450,000
General medical	100 x £1,800	180,000
TOTAL:		**1,030,000**

Exercise Six

Calculation of the additional price for the contract with Riverside PCT following additional numbers of in-patients.

		£
Current Orthopaedic contract		1,068,000

add: additional variable costs:

Drugs
£40,000/506   £79.05 × 25

         1,976

Prostheses
£100,000/506   £197.63 × 25

         $\dfrac{4,940}{6,916}$ 6,916

         1,074,916

Current ENT contract	700,000
Current General medical contract	666,000
Total: based on additional referrals (25) in Orthopaedics	**2,440,916**

Exercise Seven

Calculation of the wages and salaries budget for a new critical care unit.

(a) (i) If the unit is to open on 1st October, this is half-way through the financial year 2004/05, so the budget will include six months' salaries and wages, and not a full year.

(ii) The 2005/06 budget covers a full twelve months.

(iii) The 2005/06 budget will have a pay award of 3.225% in it.

(iv) National Insurance contributions from the employer will have to be estimated. These will be based on the number of staff, and their pay point on the scale.

(v) The setting up of the unit will require staff with specialist experience. The two Band 8A posts have been costed at the maximum point of the scale.

(vi) The staff other than the two Band 8A staff are costed at a mean of their salary range. In the local conditions of this unit, is it realistic to expect that the posts can be filled at the average level of pay?

2 Nurse consultants			Budget for		Maximum		Budget for
Band 8A			2004/05		of scale		2005/06
	Maximum		£				£
	of scale				38,709	2003/04	
	38,709	2003/04			1,248	increase	
	1,248	increase of 3.225%			39,957	2004/05	
	39,957	2004/05			1,288	increase	
					41,245	2005/06	
2 staff	79,914	Half-year	39,957		2 staff	full year	82,490
8 Specialist nurses							
Band 7					Mid-point		
	Mid-point				of scale		
	of scale				29,315	2003/04	
	29,315	2003/04			945	increase	
	945	increase			30,260	2004/05	
	30,260	2004/05			975	increase	
					31,235	2005/06	
8 staff	242,080	Half-year	121,040		8 staff	Full year	249,880
5 Qualified nurses					Mid-point		
Band 5					of scale		
	Mid-point				20,128	2003/04	
	of scale				649	increase	
	20,128	2003/04			20,777	2004/05	
	649	increase			670	increase	
	20,777	2004/05			21,447	2005/06	
5 staff	103,885	Half-year	51,943		5 staff	Full year	107,235

Exercise Seven cont'd

2 medical secretaries					Mid-point		
Band 3					of scale		
	Mid-point					14,115	2003/04
	of scale					455	increase
	14,115	2003/04				14,570	2004/05
	455	increase				470	increase
	14,570	2004/05				15,040	2005/06
2 staff	29,140	Half-year	**14,570**		2 staff	Full year	**30,080**
One half-time medical secretary							
Supervisor Band 4					Mid-point		
	Mid-point				of scale		
	of scale						
	16,541	2003/04				16,541	2003/04
	533	increase				533	increase
	17,074	2004/05				17,074	2004/05
						550	increase
Half-time	8,537	Half-year	**4,268**			17,624	2005/06
					1 staff member, half-time		
					Full year		**8,812**
	TOTAL:		**231,778**		**TOTAL:**		**478,497**

Note: in each case where 'increase' is mentioned, the basic salary has been increased by 3.225%.
This is in line with the information in the question.

Glossary of Terms

These definitions describe accounting and financial terms, and relate both to the private sector and the National Health Service.

Account A record of one or more transactions of the same type to enable a total to be ascertained, relating to a period, such as a week, a month, a year.

Accountancy The process of analysing, classifying and recording transactions in terms of time, quantity and money.

Accounting period The period for which records are kept (also known as the financial year).

Accounting system The method by which transactions are recorded and which produces summaries for use by internal management. Systems may be stand alone, based on a single department or integrated by the use of common systems across a Trust or PCT.

Accrual accounting The basis on which accounts in the private sector are prepared. This recognises a commitment at the point at which it is entered into. Consequently, if by the end of a financial period, the item has not been paid for in full, the outstanding amount is calculated, and called an 'accrual', and is added to the actual spending of that period, so that the full cost of services or goods is recorded. This is sometimes known as the 'matching principle'; where an organisation is not satisfied with a record of receipts and payments, but requires a true picture of actual levels of activity, and the costs incurred in running the organisation, which consist of both 'payments and 'accruals', that is, money which has been handed over, plus bills which are outstanding, but which relate to the financial period even though they are not paid.

Advice note A note accompanying the delivery of goods which confirms the details of the delivery (sometimes described as the despatch or delivery note).

Age analysis A term used in credit control. A schedule or list of amounts owing to an organisation, which shows the amount involved and the length of time for which the item has been unpaid.

Allocation Over the three years 2003/04 to 2005/06 the Department of Health is allocating £148.3 billions to PCTs. For the first time, revenue resources have been planned for a period of three years rather than a single year. The website explaining the process is www.doh.uk/allocations

Amortisation The writing off of the cost of a certain type of asset, for example the cost of a lease, where the expense involved is caused by the passage of time.

Analyse The process of classifying and aggregating similar types of transaction under a particular heading which describes the nature of the expenditure, for example to collect together all gas bills under the heading 'heating and lighting'.

Asset Goods, resources and property of all kinds which the business or organisation intends to keep for the purpose of running the business.

Audit An independent examination of the accounts and records maintained by an organisation, to establish whether stated policies have been carried out, and to express an opinion on the state of the records.

Auditor The person who conducts the audit.

Balance (noun) The difference which exists between two sides of an account, which represents the present state of that account.

Balance (verb) To prepare a total for both sides of an account, and to calculate the difference, or the resulting figure, which represents the excess of one side over the other.

Balance sheet A financial statement showing the assets, liabilities and capital at a financial year end, indicating to the owners, shareholders or other interested parties the financial state of the organisation in terms of what it owns and what it owes at that particular time.

Bank reconciliation The process of listing unpresented cheques and deposits which have not yet shown up on a bank statement, and adjusting for differences between the records kept by the customer, and by the bank, so that both records agree.

Book keeping The technique of keeping accounts; of recording in a regular, concise and accurate way the transactions of an organisation or a business.

Capacity planning The DoH has prepared a model to assist local authorities to plan services for older people. It allows authorities to compare their planned growth with their expected share in the growth of national capacity. See www.doh.gov.uk/changeagentteam/capacityplanningmodel

Capital The initial starting amount of money in a business or enterprise, put in by the owners or their financial supporters in order for the business to acquire the assets or resources with which to run the business. Capital represents the stake in the business attributable to the owners. It is increased by profits, and reduced by withdrawals taken by the owners. In a limited company situation, capital may be 'subscribed' by shareholders, and the value of their stake will fluctuate according to the fortunes of the company. The withdrawals are taken in the form of dividends. In the National Health Service, the capital needed to run the scale of the service is provided from the proceeds of national taxation, and the growth of the service depends on the amounts decided by Parliament in the annual review of expenditure. Capital in the context of health authorities is a cash sum made available by the Department of Health through the Treasury, and represents a direct investment by central government in health facilities. In a Trust situation, capital is inherited from predecessor authorities and the burden of debt associated with those assets becomes the responsibility of the trust to finance.

Capitation-based funding Each region's population is weighted to reflect demands placed on health services by different age groups. These rates are based on the estimated expenditure per head for different age groups. These age-weighted populations are adjusted by the standardised mortality rate. Certain geographical supplements are built into the allocations, for example special funds for London due to the predominance of teaching hospitals, and the prevalence of certain types of illness.

Care pathway   A means of determining locally agreed, multidisciplinary health practice, based on guidelines and evidence for a specific user group. They forecast the sequence of procedures, provide a means of managing clinical procedures, and patient outcomes, and form all or part of the clinical record, documenting the care given.

Cash flow   Part of the business plan, or business case for a new development, to identify the cash required and to forecast the timing of receipts and payments, so that where income is delayed, the timing of borrowings or the drawing down of cash from the DoH can be arranged to finance the organisation or department.

Cash limit   A financial term which was used in government accounting prior to the introduction of the resource accounting and budgeting system in 2001. It has now largely been replaced by the term 'resource limit', which refers to revenue allocations made to health organisations, for example PCTs.

Charitable funds   Money held by a department or an organisation which has been provided for a designated purpose, for example, the provision of patients' amenities, and to which the rules of the Charities Act apply.

Close off/ close down   To carry out the final accounting entries relating to a financial period; to transfer details of expenditure and income to an annual statement (the revenue account in the case of the public sector, and the profit and loss account in the case of the private sector).

Commissioning   The development of purchasing strategies to make the best use of all available resources to meet identified needs, both in the short and the long term, bringing together financial and service planning.

Contra   A Latin word meaning 'against'. The matching of one item against another: for example, cancelling a debt due from one person, by setting against it an amount which is due to that person. One entry cancels out the other hence 'contra'.

Core services   Those services, such as accident and emergency services, to which patients need local access and where there is no sensible alternative provision available.

Corporate governance	The system by which the organisation is directed and controlled, at its most senior levels, in order to achieve its objectives and meet the necessary standards of accountability and probity. Effective corporate governance, along with clinical governance, is essential for a PCT to achieve its clinical and quality and financial directives. Fundamental to effective corporate governance is having the means to identify the effectiveness of this direction and control. This is achieved through what the NHS calls 'controls assurance'. See Corporate Governance Framework For Primary Care Trusts www.doh.gov.uk/pct/pctcgver34.doc
Cost and volume contracts	The provider recovers a sum in return for treating a specified number of cases.
Cost centre	An expenditure code attached to a particular department, function or service in an organisation, which can be used to identify the total costs incurred within an accounting period by that department's function or service.
Cost per case contracts	The purchaser agrees the price to be paid for the treatment of individual patients.
Cost pressure	Where the budget allowance made is unlikely to be sufficient to meet expenditure, due to increased costs (from external sources) such as higher unit costs of drugs, or where the level of activity is much higher than anticipated (for example the effects of a harsh period of weather on accelerating the rate of referrals to a fracture clinic). Managers or budget holders are said to be experiencing 'cost pressure'.
Credit (noun)	An entry on the right-hand side of a ledger.
Credit (verb)	To 'credit' is to make an entry on the right-hand side.
Credit note	A document sent to a person, firm or organisation, confirming that the account is credited with the amount stated (for example when goods are returned by that person, firm and so on, or when an allowance is made to that person, firm and so on).
Creditor	One to whom money is owed for supplies, goods, services and so on.
Current assets	A description covering a group of different things which are assets in a reasonably realisable state: for example bank balances, cash, stores, stock items, debtors and so on.

Debit (noun)	An entry on the left-hand side of a ledger account.
Debit (verb)	To 'debit' an account is to make an entry on the left-hand side.
Debit note	A document sent to a person, company and so on, stating that their account has been charged with the amount stated. For example, goods ordered by phone, and for which the debit note acts as confirmation that the items have been charged to the person or organisation from whom the order emanated.
Debtor	A person who owes money for goods, or services supplied but not paid for.
Depreciation	The estimated loss in value of an asset due to its use, and charged as a deduction or charge against revenues of a particular period.
Discount	A deduction from the amount due under an invoice; for example a trade discount is an allowance granted to a purchaser who is entitled to some special treatment by the supplier, for example a supplier of lighting fittings may grant a trade discount to those firms which regularly stock their products, and the difference between the catalogue or selling price and the price of the item to the purchaser represents the 'trade discount'.

A 'settlement discount' is a reduction in the size of the final bill as a 'thank you' for prompt or early settlement of the bill. |
Endowment funds	Derived from donations or from legacies, and must be used in accordance with the express purposes of the fund.
Extra-contractual referrals	These are known as ECRs. They represent non-predictable referrals, either emergency or non-emergency. Purchasers are obliged to pay for emergency treatments, but for non-emergency cases the provider is required to obtain approval from the purchaser before the treatment commences.
Final accounts	The statements prepared to summarise and record the results of a financial period.
Financial flows	The DoH issued a Consultation Paper in October 2002 *Reforming NHS Financial Flows: Introducing payments by results.* It is intended that from 2005/06 a national tariff will be introduced for six surgical specialties,

and there will be 15 designated HRGs (health care resource groups) where payment will be made by financing these activities on a cost per case. See www.doh.gov.uk/nhsfinancialreforms

Fixed asset   An asset which is in permanent use within a firm, company, business or organisation.

Fixed cost   Fixed costs remain unchanged as output or activity increases. For example, if an ambulance Trust rented a garage for overnight storage of vehicles, the cost of that expenditure would be regarded as a fixed cost, as whether there were two, or five or no ambulances in the garage, the rent would still be the same figure in terms of outgoings of the Trust to the landlord. If, at a later date, new vehicles were ordered, and more garaging was needed, then there would be a second amount of fixed cost added to the original level. If costs rise in this way, they are known as 'stepped costs'.

Franchise plan   This is a document, prepared by a Chief Executive of a Strategic Health Authority, which sets out for one year in detail, and in outline for a further two years how the Chief Executive will deliver improvements in the quality of health care, responsiveness to the needs of patients and local communities, and the health status of the population served, in line with the requirements of the NHS Plan. See www.doh.gov.uk/shiftingthe balance/nextstepsaapb

Gross   A total without any deductions, for example 'gross pay' is the total amount of pay a person is entitled to, before taking off any deductions.

Grossing up   The calculation of a gross figure from a net figure by adding on the deductions already made in arriving at the net figure.

Impersonal accounts   Accounts not dealing with persons but other things, for example 'real' accounts containing details of property, and 'nominal' accounts dealing with expenses and revenues.

Imprest system   A method in which a predetermined sum is given to a budget holder for small items of expenditure, and these outgoings are periodically reimbursed so that the imprest holder has the amount of cash restored to the original level.

Intangible asset   An asset which is neither fixed nor current yet which possesses an intrinsic value, for example a brand name.

Inventory   A listing of items owned by an organisation, usually applied to stock, and to which values are applied, so that the organisation can trace its own assets.

Invoice   A document showing the character, quantity, price, terms, address for delivery and other particulars of goods sold or services supplied.

Journal   A means of recording transactions which is commonly used in the health service for adjustments of money between departments. Journal transfers are internal adjustments which obviate the need to draw a cheque, as the transfer of money is within the same organisation.

Large capital   Are controlled by StHAs and PCTs and cover
schemes   major building work and medical equipment costing over £50,000.

Ledger   A collection of accounts. A general ledger contains a summary of all the principal accounts which form the basis of the annual accounts. A creditors' ledger contains details of transactions with suppliers, and a debtors' ledger contains details of transactions affecting customers.

Ledger account   A record in the ledger showing one of the two aspects of each transaction or group of transactions.

Liabilities   A general heading under which are recorded amounts owing to suppliers (creditors), expenses (accruals) and debts owing by the firm or organisation.

Liquidity   The excess of cash or current assets over current liabilities. ('Current' in this context means repayable within the next 12 months.)

Local delivery   These will:
plans   • Set out short, medium and long-term service development plans within both the local and national strategic context
                        • Set out the service issues which will be addressed, supporting capacity changes, and the affordability of proposals
                        • Demonstrate how service levels and costs will change over the period, coupled with the milestones

	and monitoring arrangements to assess progress towards these levels ● Identify risks to delivery and put in place agreed contingency arrangements to ensure objectives are met ● See www.doh.gov.uk/nhsfinancialreforms/sla_guidance
Materiality	A consideration of the significance of an amount in relation to the context in which it is placed. In relation to accounts, an amount is not material if its effect on the accounts would not distort the overall truth and fairness of the view they give.
Minor capital schemes	Are controlled by Strategic Health Authorities, Trusts and PCTs, and are in respect of: ● medical equipment ● vehicles ● minor building work and alterations ● fire precautions ● staff accommodation ● other similar schemes.
Net	The amount of any charge or cost after all deductions have been taken out.
Nominal accounts	Accounts for the income (and expenses) of an organisation.
Nominal ledger	An alternative term for the general ledger.
Non-core services	Those services for which health authorities have scope for exercising choice.
Performance indicators	Measurable numerical indicators of performance set by the government, the Audit Commission or local authorities.
Personal account	An account showing transactions with a particular person, firm or company, as distinct from a nominal account.
Petty cash	A system for dealing with small payments, in which a budget holder or similarly authorised person is given a small amount of funds out of which minor payments can be made. Periodically, the fund is replenished up to the original amount, by reimbursing expenditure. This is known as the 'imprest' system of petty cash.
Posting	The transfer of entries from one record to another.

Prepayment	A payment made in the accounting period which relates to goods or services of a future period. For example, an insurance premium usually lasts for a full year. If part of the premium goes beyond the financial year end, then that part is regarded as a prepayment.
Profit and loss account	A summary account of all the revenue and expenses for a period, and the difference between income and expenditure for that period.
Provider role	To deliver contracted services within quality and quantity specifications to one or a number of purchasers in return for agreed charges.
Provisions (as an expense)	A term which is used as a description for the purchase of food for use within an organisation; for example in a hospital, provisions indicates the cost of meat, flour, fish and groceries, which are then converted into meals.
Provisions (in the context of final accounts)	Amounts written off or retained out of profits to provide for the depreciation, renewal or diminution of assets, or retained to provide for any known liability of which the amount cannot be determined with accuracy.
Purchasing role	Within available resources, services are secured to meet the health needs of the purchaser's resident population.
Reconcile (verb)	To ascertain the precise components of the difference between two related figures produced independently of each other.
Reconciliation	A statement showing the process whereby the balances of two accounts, which have been prepared in respect of the same transactions, have been agreed. For example, a bank reconciliation compares the records kept by the organisation with the records or statement provided by the bank, and agrees the two by allowing for timing differences in the depositing of money and the presentation of cheques.
Revenue	Income received or generated from any source.
Schedule	A detailed list of items totalled to agree with a figure that has been analysed and cross-referenced.
Semi-variable costs	Costs which are partly fixed, and partly vary with usage, for example a telephone bill is fixed in regard to the line rental charge, and variable in relation to the call charges.

Statement of account	An account, periodically rendered, showing the amounts due by one person or firm to another. Generally, a statement contains only the dates and amounts of each invoice sent since the previous settlement.
Stock	The value of items which have been acquired but not used, for example amounts of stationery, drugs, dressings and provisions. These are usually valued at the lower of cost or net realisable value.
Suspense account	An unexplained item or series of items, which are temporarily not included in the accounts until their exact nature has been discovered.
Total (or control) accounts	An account which acts as a summary of all the items debited or credited to a number of individual accounts in a ledger, so that the total account may represent the individual accounts in providing a single figure in summary instead of a whole series of figures. A total or control account is often used in payroll, to check the accuracy of a great number of transactions before the final net pay is released from the organisation. Total accounts support the work which has been done in detail, and are complementary to the detailed work. They are a means of proving the accuracy of detailed work in an independent way.
Transfer	An amount taken from one account and reinstated in another.
Trial balance	A summary listing all the balances in a ledger.
Turnover	The total sales or revenue generated by a business or organisation.
Variable costs	Those costs which increase as the number of patients or type of activity increases. Thus, the cost of plaster in a fracture clinic will increase proportionately to the number of new patients handled by the clinic. Some costs will not alter according to the number of patients, and these should be excluded from the variable costs; for example heating and lighting will be the same and will not vary with throughput of patients.
Weighted capitation formula	The Department of Health allocates revenue funding to PCTs on the basis of the relative needs of their populations. A weighted capitation formula determines each PCT's target share of available resources to

enable them to commission similar levels of health services for populations in similar levels of need. The formula is described in a DoH booklet: *Resource Allocation-Weighted Capitation Formula.* Web site: www.doh.gov.uk/allocations/formula.

Writing off   The closing of an account or part of an account by charging debt to the revenue account, or profit and loss account, as irrecoverable. Strict rules governing the circumstances in which amounts can be written off are usually in place in an authority's financial regulations, to avoid the loss of money through unauthorised cancellation of amounts owing.

Writing up   Increasing the value of an asset by making appropriate entries in the books of account.

Further Advanced Reading

Texts

For readers who wish to take the subject further, these texts contain discussion and illustrations of health service finance, and capital and revenue budgeting.

Bailey D (1994) *The NHS Budget Holder's Survival Guide*, The Royal Society of Medicine Press, London

Chartered Institute of Public Finance and Accountancy (2003) *Financial Control and Budgeting for NHS Partnerships*, CIPFA, London.

Chartered Institute of Public Finance and Accountancy (2001) *Health Service Value for Money Guide – Volume 1 and Volume 2*, CIPFA, London.

Coombs HM and Jenkins DE (1996) *Public Sector Financial Management*, 2nd edn, International Thomson Business Press, London.

Doherty TL and Horne T (2002) *Managing Public Services, Implementing Changes – A Thoughtful Approach*, Routledge, London. Chapters 9 & 10, Managing Budgets in Public Services, and Managing Resources in Public Services 282–325.

Doyle D (1994) *Cost Control: A Strategic Guide*, Kogan Page, London.

Drury C (1996) *Management and Cost Accounting*, 4th edn, International Thomson Business Press, London.

Glynn JJ, Perrin J and Murphy MP (1995) *Accounting for Managers*, Chapman & Hall, London.

Jackson PM and Lavender M (1997) *The Public Services Yearbook*, Pitman Publishing, London. (Annual).

Jones B (1996) *Financial Management in the Public Sector*, McGraw-Hill, Maidenhead.

Jones R and Pendlebury M (1996) *Public Sector Accounting*, 4th edn, Pitman Publishing, London.

Mellett H, Marriott N and Harries S (1993) *Financial Management in the NHS: A Manager's Handbook*. Chapman & Hall, London.

Scottish Office, National Health Service in Scotland Management Executive (1996) *NHS Trusts: Guidance for Finance Managers*. HMSO, Edinburgh.

Research Papers

Bourne M and Sutcliffe C (eds) (1996) *Management Accounting in Healthcare*, The Chartered Institute of Management Accountants, London.

Chartered Institute of Public Finance and Accountancy (2001) *Accountability – A Framework for Primary Care Trusts*, CIPFA, London.

Chartered Institute of Public Finance and Accountancy (2003) *Payment by Results: New Financial Flows in the NHS in England*, CIPFA, London.

Ellwood S (2001) *Accruals Accounting Approaches in the Uk Public Sector: Diversity and Convergence* International Comparative Issues in Government Accounting (Proceedings of the 7th CIGAR Conference) Bac, A (Editor), Kluwer Academic Publishers, Dordrecht, The Netherlands.

Lapsley I, Llewellyn S and Burnett G (1998) *Inside Hospital Trusts: Management Styles, Accounting Constraints*, The Institute of Chartered Accountants of Scotland, Edinburgh. (Research report).

Purdey DE (1994) *Cash Budgets and the Psychology of Managing Healthcare in the NHS*, Discussion papers in accounting, finance and banking, No. 39, University of Reading, Department of Economics, Reading.

Sutcliffe CMS (1997) *Developing Decision Support Systems: A Study of Healthcare Management*, The Chartered Institute of Management Accountants, London.

Magazine Articles and Journals

Bailey D (1995) Getting your money's worth out of your accountant, *British Journal of Health Care Management*, 3(4): 215–17.

Bailey D (1995) Take control of your budget, Nursing Management, 1(8): 16–17.

Bailey D (1995) Wage war on your budget, *Nursing Management*, 1(9): 22–3.

Bailey D (1996) Budgeting skills, *Nursing Standard*, 10: 43–6.

Cavouras CA and McKinley J (1997) Variable budgeting for staffing: analysis and evaluation, *Nursing Management* (US), 28(5): 34, 36, 39.

Cook A (1995) Management accounting, *British Medical Journal*, 310: 381–5.

Craske C (1997) Cash control, *Nursing Times*, 93: 69–71.

Foot P (2004) A Guide to the Private Finance Initiative: a special report in P.F. Eye *Private Eye*, 1102, March 19 2004, 1–11.

Hunter D (2003) Foundation Hospitals: Back to the Future, *Public Money and Management*, 23(4): 211–13.

Lapsley I (1994) Responsibility accounting revived? Market reforms and budgetary control in healthcare, *Management Accounting Research*, 5(3/4): 337–52.

Likierman A (2003) Planning and Controlling UK Public Expenditure on a Resource Basis, *Public Money and Management*, 23(1): 45–51.

Marriott DN and Mellett HJ (1995) The level of skills of National Health Service managers, *Financial Accountability and Management*, **11**(3): 271–82.

Marriott N and Mellett H (1996) Perceived quality of management information and the influence of overspending penalties in the NHS, *Health Services Management Research*, **9**(4): 254–61.

Murphy MP and Perkins DA (1995) Devolved budgetary management systems: means, ends, or myth? *British Journal of Health Care Management*, **1**(6): 283–5.

Pilkington S (1997) Year to end budget forecasting, income and expenditure, *British Journal of Hospital Medicine*, **57**(10): 527–30.

Plumridge N (2003) Payment by Numbers, *Public Finance* September 19 2003, 20–23.

Sengin KK and Dreisbach AM (1995) Managing with precision: a budgetary decision support model, *Journal of Nursing Administration* (US), **25**(2): 33–44.

Woodgates P (1995) Multiple division, *Health Service Journal*, **105**: 28–30

Index